WALK THROUGH THE WALL, AMERICA

How We Can Stop Federal Judges From Dictating Our Laws Without Our Approval

By Mark Sutton

A LEGAL WATCH PUBLICATION ™

PRESS

Walk Through the Wall, America
by Mark Sutton

Printed in the United States of America

ISBN 1-597811-16-5

www.xulonpress.com

TABLE OF CONTENTS

ACKNOWLEDGEMENTS

There are many people to thank for helping in this project. The first and foremost thanks go to my family, namely my wife, Christine, and my five sons, Paul, Joel, David, Daniel and Andrew. They had to put up with my absence, either physically or mentally, for hundreds of hours while I wrote (and rewrote) this book. Christine, Paul and Joel also provided helpful suggestions that were implemented. For example, a substantial part of the hypothetical story in the "Prologue" was Christine's idea.

Second, my thanks go to Tam Thanh Pham, an associate attorney at our law office. She engaged with me in many hours of discussions about virtually all of the issues in this book. She also did a substantial amount of excellent legal and factual research, as well as provided many helpful suggestions for all aspects of this book. For example, two of the hypothetical stories were primarily her ideas.

Third, I express gratitude to my secretary, Gwen Simmons. She not only did numerous and seemingly endless revisions, she provided several suggestions that were implemented. I initially declined to implement some, but, as usual, she was correct in the end.

Special thanks go to my partner, John Park, who patiently allowed me the flexibility to write this book. He also gave me some good pointers. Others at our firm also provided helpful suggestions including another secretary who did many revisions, Mindy Choi. An associate attorney at our firm, Anna Nam, and a law clerk, Chong Roh also gave useful suggestions.

It was not my original idea to write a book about the law. That happened only after I received suggestions from Myrna Guttierez and Marylou Martinez. My thanks also go to Dick Mills, who gave me further motivation to write. I needed that because a practicing attorney typically cannot envision the time to write a book.

Special gratitude goes to Molly Sutherland and her ministry, Resurrected Life Ministries. Absent her ministry to my family, this effort would, in all likelihood, never have been started, let alone finished.

Thanks also go to many others who made significant contributions to this book by reviewing the manuscript. Louise May and my wife, Christine, thought of the title of this book without, at the time, understanding its full meaning. The somewhat mysterious meaning is explained in Chapter One. Louise also gave other thoughtful suggestions. The list of others who also reviewed portions of the manuscript and provided input includes (I hope I am not missing anyone): Bob Kennedy, George Giese, Brian Howes, Alice Roh and Sue Ahn. Finally, Dana Kincer and my wife, Christine, also helped with the front cover design.

It should be understood that the ideas (and any mistakes) in this book are mine alone. Neither my law firm, nor any individuals have endorsed the opinions expressed. I also acknowledge that I am not infallible and reserve the right to change my opinions in the future.

PREFACE

This book addresses issues raised by judicial law-making, assuming no knowledge of the law. By making constitutional law, federal judges can by-pass democracy and, in many respects, rule America from the judicial bench. The issue of judges creating constitutional law has been raised by recent legal cases such as those involving Ten Commandments displays, same-sex marriage and partial birth abortion.

Some federal judges have repeatedly and without any fear of consequences effectively amended the U.S. Constitution for more than fifty years. The resulting judge-made constitutional amendments are unconstitutional acts, because judges are not permitted by the Constitution to make constitutional law.

Unconstitutional acts by Congress and the President can be declared to have no effect by the U.S. Supreme Court. Therefore, the U.S. Supreme Court checks the power of Congress and the President, as do the American people through elections. However, there is no way for the other branches of the federal government, or the people of America, to stop unconstitutional actions by the U.S. Supreme Court.

The U.S. Constitution is the "supreme" law of the

United States. Therefore, judge-made constitutional amend
ments cannot be corrected, unless the Supreme Court
decides to correct them, or a constitutional amendment is
ratified by three-quarters of the fifty states to correct them.

Many people believe that the appropriate solution to this
problem is for the President to appoint federal judges who
voluntarily stay within the limits of their judicial power.
However, in recent decades, many Supreme Court justices
have been appointed by Presidents with that solution in
mind, but those same justices have proceeded to repeatedly
engage in judicial law-making. This is possible because, as
mentioned above, there is no way for the other branches of
the federal government to stop the U.S. Supreme Court from
making new constitutional law. Thus, attempting to appoint
judges to the Supreme court who will not exceed their
power has proven to be of limited effectiveness in prevent-
ing judicial law-making.

There is another remedy in the Constitution to prevent a
"despotism of the oligarchy" of federal judges, as it was
described by the primary author of the Declaration of
Independence, Thomas Jefferson. That remedy is impeachment and removal of judges who violate the U.S.
Constitution. This will at least stop a particular judge from
violating the Constitution in the future. I believe the
American people should take back their right of self-
government by requiring the President to appoint judges
who will refrain from making constitutional law, and by
requiring Congress to consider removing law-making
federal judges from office.

The primary example of a judge-made constitutional
amendment discussed here is the "separation of church and
state" doctrine. In 1947, that doctrine was injected into the
First Amendment. The "separation of church and state"
doctrine is not in the actual language of the First
Amendment, which simply says: "Congress shall make no

law respecting an establishment of religion." The "separation of church and state" concept is a much stronger prohibition than the above-quoted Establishment Clause. Therefore, by injecting the "separation of church and state" concept into the Establishment Clause, the U.S. Supreme Court effectively amended the First Amendment without the required democratic process.

The Establishment Clause of the First Amendment was designed to, among other things, *prevent the new federal government from interfering* with the religious practices of the state and local governments. In 1947, the Establishment Clause was altered to mean, in many respects, the opposite of what it originally meant. According to the U.S. Supreme Court, the Establishment Clause now means that *the federal government must interfere* with most interfaces between religion and state governments.

The U.S. Supreme Court, and sometimes lower federal courts have expanded the judge-made "separation of church and state" doctrine in recent decades. In expanding that doctrine, the federal courts often limit the free exercise of religion and the freedom of speech, rights that are expressly protected by the First Amendment. Therefore, for those and other reasons, some federal judges should be considered for impeachment and removal from office.

PROLOGUE:
A HYPOTHETICAL STORY

†〓〓†

Theresa Collins, a young woman of twenty-five years, had started as the principal's secretary at St. Ruth's Elementary School in Kirkbride, Missouri only five days earlier. She had moved to the mid-western city to get away from the threat of violence she had experienced in New York City.

At the school that day, the sounds were horrific-gunshots followed by angry yelling, sounds that would never leave Theresa Collins' mind. The sounds of the children screaming with terror were magnified in her mind, as if they had been broadcasted on the P.A. system of the school. As utter chaos hit St. Ruth's, the teachers tried to calm the children down, but the angry young men who planned to make an example of middle America were too loud. Some of the children would not stop crying.

Theresa crawled along the floor to the phone on her desk and called 911. The operator tried to calm her down and said help was already on the way.

* * *

When he arrived at St. Ruth's, Captain Tom Gridley found eight other police officers already at the scene. He could tell others were coming because he could hear the sirens in the distance.

"What's goin' on?" Tom asked one of the officers. Sgt. George Clipton responded, "We have a hostage situation. Eight to ten armed men have taken the teachers and students hostage in the assembly hall of the school. I don't think they speak English."

Tom ordered, "Surround the school so that no one escapes." "Yes, sir," said George as he proceeded to obey Tom's order.

Tom got on his car radio again. "Give me the Chief," Tom demanded. Police Chief Wesley Rogers got on the radio and asked, "What's the situation?"

Tom replied, "We have cordoned off the school on the streets. About twenty units have arrived with others on the way. So far, I haven't seen anyone. George told me that the students and teachers have been taken hostage in the assembly hall of the school."

"We have a problem about how to handle this situation," the Chief responded. "As I told everyone at the briefing earlier this week, we're not supposed to provide police or fire services to religious organizations because of the lawsuit."

Tom said, "I can't believe that the lawsuit applies to this situation."

"I hope you're right. I'll call the City Attorney right now." The Chief terminated radio contact.

* * *

About ten minutes later, Chief Rogers called Tom's car radio. He told Tom, "I've spoken to the City Attorney. He told me that if we do anything while the suspects are on school property, we'll be violating the court order. Last week the Supreme Court determined that the order will stand, so our hands are tied as long as the terrorists stay on school property. Our attorney said that the 'separation of church and state' doctrine requires us to remain separate from all activities on school property."

Tom replied, "I hear you, but I still can't believe it. Are you sure?"

"That's what he told me. The City is two million dollars in the red because of the lawsuit. The opposing attorneys told our attorneys that if the City violates the order, the City, as well as the personnel involved, will be in contempt of court. The Mayor made it clear that we'll lose our jobs, and may be put in jail, if we violate the order," the Chief emphasized.

"Wait! An armed man's leading the students and teachers out onto the playground. I think we should concentrate most of the personnel near the playground and have our weapons trained on the suspects. What do you think?"

"I think you're right, but don't open fire unless I give you the command," instructed the Chief.

Tom relayed the Chief's instructions to George and put George in charge of the officers near the playground.

After a few minutes, Tom spoke to the Chief again. "Chief, I wanna have you on the radio for immediate access as events happen. Right now, the students and teachers are all lying on the playground. Three of the suspects are talking."

The Chief said, "Alright, I want you to take out your bull horn and demand that the suspects lay down their weapons and walk to the street with their hands up." Tom followed orders but the terrorists ignored him.

Suddenly, the terrorists began shooting the students and teachers. "Sir, they're shooting 'em... should we open fire?" Tom implored.

The Chief replied, "I wanna say yes, but I can't! I don't like this any more than you do!" The terrorists quickly shot the students and teachers. Some of the students and teachers attempted to flee. They were gunned down before they could reach the street.

* * *

It seemed like hours as Theresa waited for help, though in actuality it was only about twenty minutes. Then she heard a rapid fire of gunshots, like popcorn, over the shrill cries of the innocent children. After a few minutes, the children's cries decreased, as did the repetitiveness of the gunshots. Then there was silence.

* * *

After the executions were completed, the terrorists opened the back door of their van, pulled out some red containers and began pouring gasoline onto the base of the school buildings. Tom described the events to the Chief, who ordered the dispatcher to call the fire department.

By the time the fire trucks arrived at the scene, the terrorists finished emptying their containers and began igniting the fuel. Soon, the school buildings were engulfed in flames.

* * *

Theresa made another attempt to call 911, but the phone lines were obviously too busy. That's when she smelled the stench of gasoline. It was everywhere! Then she could smell smoke. Heat was coming through the walls and a cloud of smoke began to seep under the doors.

Theresa found her purse under her desk. She crawled to the door by the teachers' parking lot and saw her co-worker Mary Tambown bloodied and lying facedown on the welcome mat. In an adrenaline rush, Theresa stood up and ran for her car. Because she had arrived at work early that morning, her car was close to the door. Theresa clenched the keys she took from her pocket and didn't look back as she ran to her car.

Theresa quickly started the car and drove it out of the parking lot to Lina's Family Market down the street. There, she could see a line of police cars and fire engines parked along the road. Only then, did she turn around to see the bodies and her school, her new school of only five days, ablaze in flames.

One hundred forty-seven students. Theresa knew the exact number of attendees that day, because she kept the attendance records. That was part of her job, her peaceful job, in a quiet mid-western city. Why Kirkbride, Missouri? Why anywhere? Why didn't the police just shoot the terrorists? How could all those firemen stand by and watch an entire set of school buildings burn to the ground?

* * *

The terrorists threw their weapons on the ground and piled into the van. Tom described the events to the Chief and asked, "Should we arrest them when they get to the street?" The Chief replied, "Only if they have weapons or if they break any other laws when they leave school property. I want two cars to tail 'em. I'll call the state troopers. Since they're not subject to the court order, maybe they'll arrest 'em."

The terrorists backed out onto the street and drove away with two police cars trailing after them. When they reached the city limits, the state troopers were waiting. They arrested the terrorists. The Kirkbride police cars returned to the station.

Meanwhile, the Chief arrived at St. Ruth's and saw the devastation. He was a burly six-two, but he couldn't stop weeping when he saw the bodies. The Chief's own childhood flashed before him. The tears now flowed down his face as he remembered Pastor Danson's prayers for him to be a protector of people in danger, after he had told the cleric his intention of becoming a policeman. How could this have happened?

* * *

The Chief had to face the media. They demanded to know why the police and fire department stood by and did nothing to stop the terrorists. He explained that the police and fire departments were subject to a federal court order which required them to remain "separate" from St. Ruth's, because it was a religious school. With tears streaming down his face, he said that he wanted to order his men to shoot the terrorists before they carried out the executions, but that would have violated the court order.

CHAPTER 1

AN INTRODUCTION TO JUDICIAL TYRANNY

The hypothetical story in the "Prologue" dramatically illustrates the kind of problem that can result from federal judges unconstitutionally changing the U.S. Constitution.

An Example Of The Problem: The "Separation Of Church And State" Doctrine

In a case called Everson v. Ewing Township Board of Education (1947),[1] the U.S. Supreme Court determined for the first time that the First Amendment to the U.S. Constitution required a "wall of separation between church and state." The U.S. Supreme Court did that even though those words are not in the First Amendment, and there was no other constitutional provision that provided those words.

In a later case, Brandon v. Guilderland Central School District (1980),[2] the Second Circuit Court of Appeals stated that a "strict reading" of the "separation of church and state" doctrine would require local governments to deny police and fire protection to religious schools and organizations. The foregoing hypothetical story illustrates what the Brandon Court referred to as the "strict reading" of the "separation of church and state" doctrine, even though the Brandon Court also said that the "separation of church and state" doctrine should not be "strictly" applied.

My reason for providing the foregoing hypothetical story in the "Prologue" is not to suggest that these circumstances are likely to become a reality in America's future. I do not want to believe, or in fact believe, that such things will happen in America some day. My reason for including these hypothetical circumstances is to graphically illustrate that the judge-made "separation of church and state" doctrine is a *much broader and stronger prohibition* than the actual language of the First Amendment's Establishment Clause.

The actual language of the Establishment Clause provides that "Congress shall make no law respecting an establishment of religion . . . ." Even a "strict-reading" of that language could not lead to circumstances remotely similar to the foregoing hypothetical story.

On the other hand, the concept expressed by the words "wall of separation between church and state" can be reasonably understood to yield the aforementioned hypothetical events. If there in fact is a "high and impregnable" wall between government and religion, as the Everson Court said, people engaging in at least partly religious activities could be denied fire and police protection, as the Brandon Court suggested. A legal doctrine that can, in a "strict" application, lead to that result should not be part of our nation's constitutional law. But it is at the present time.

In 1947, the U.S. Supreme Court injected the "separation of church and state" concept into the Establishment Clause *without any democratic process whatsoever.* An amendment of the U.S. Constitution requires approval of three-quarters of the states. Therefore, the Establishment Clause was unconstitutionally changed (i.e., amended) by the U.S. Supreme Court. This and similar practices by our federal courts are a form of dictatorship for which there *is* a meaningful remedy in the U.S. Constitution. All of these issues, including the "separation of church and state" doctrine, are explained in detail below.

Recent Court Decisions That Also Raise The Problems Discussed In This Book

The "separation of church and state" doctrine is not the only area of constitutional law in which our federal courts have bypassed democracy. The federal courts have repeatedly made constitutional law for more than a half-century. Some federal court decisions from very recent years that are examples of judicial law-making will be briefly discussed in this section. The court decisions mentioned in this section would have been widely considered to be inconceivable only 35 to 40 years ago.

There has recently been much debate in America about whether to ratify a constitutional amendment that would require government-recognized marriage to be only between a man and a woman. This has occurred in response to state court decisions requiring some state governments to officially recognize same-sex marriage, or same-sex domestic partnerships.

During the same time period, the U.S. Supreme Court struck down as unconstitutional a Texas law making homosexual sodomy a criminal offense in a legal case called Lawrence v. Texas (2003).[3] Legal cases are named after the first-named parties in the lawsuit.

In their dissenting opinion (i.e., the minority, losing opinion) in the Lawrence case, three U.S. Supreme Court justices stated that the majority opinion is the first step toward requiring all state and federal governments in America to recognize same-sex marriage on constitutional grounds. The dissenting justices stated as follows:

"At the end of its opinion – after having laid waste to

the foundations of our rational-basis jurisprudence – the Court says that the present case 'does not involve whether the government must give formal recognition to any relationship that homosexual persons seek to enter.' . . . Do not believe it. . . . This case 'does not involve' the issue of homosexual marriage only if one entertains the belief that principle and logic have nothing to do with the decisions of this Court." [4]

A U.S. Supreme Court decision forcing homosexual marriage on the states through the U.S. Constitution would not only be an illegal amendment to the Constitution, it would overrule state initiatives restricting marriage to a man and a woman. During the November 2004 elections, such initiatives were passed by overwhelming majorities in eleven states.

During the last ten years, partial-birth abortion (i.e., the abortion of babies/fetuses who have partly emerged from the birth canal) has been a subject of much political controversy. President Bill Clinton vetoed three bills restricting partial birth abortion that were passed by Congress. President George W. Bush signed a similar bill into law, but it was declared unconstitutional and thus of no effect by a federal court. More than 30 states have democratically passed laws restricting partial birth abortions. All of those laws were also overturned by the federal courts.[5] This occurred even though some legal experts who support abortion agree that the right to an abortion is not found in the U.S. Constitution.

A U.S. Court of Appeals also decided in 2002, that the words "under God" in the pledge of allegiance were unconstitutional, if recited in public schools.[6] During 2004, the U.S. Supreme Court vacated that decision on the ground that the person who brought the lawsuit did not have the right to bring it.[7] The Supreme Court, therefore, did not decide whether the "under God" portion of the pledge of allegiance is constitutional in the public schools under the "separation of church and state" doctrine. A new case on that issue is expected to reach the U.S. Supreme Court in the future.

Also during 2003, Chief Justice Roy Moore of the Supreme Court of Alabama was involuntarily removed from office, because he refused to take down a Ten Commandments monument erected in front of the Alabama Supreme Court building. A federal court had ordered him to do so because the monument supposedly violated a legal test derived from the "separation of church and state" doctrine. These events received extensive publicity across the nation. Two cases related to Justice Moore's actions are discussed below in Chapter Nine. Two other cases involving Ten Commandments displays which are now pending before the U.S. Supreme Court are also discussed below.

The foregoing court cases, and other recent cases, have raised concerns among the American public about the abuse of power by federal judges. That problem is discussed extensively below.

The Background Circumstances That Led To This Book

The problems discussed in this book have been a significant concern of mine since I began studying law. While in law school, I read cases in which the courts went beyond the limits of their power to engage in law-making. This occurred in many areas of law, but was most pervasive and troublesome in constitutional law. The U.S. Constitution does not permit judges to make law. Furthermore, constitutional law cannot be changed without approval of three-quarters of the states, or a change of mind by the members of the U.S. Supreme Court. Since judges are not subject to elections, the American people were effectively being denied the right to govern themselves in areas where the federal courts decided to make constitutional law.

Although some of the laws made by federal judges seemed to be wise, what these judges were doing was unconstitutional. Since the American people have no right to vote for judges and have no right to remove judges from office through elections, America's constitutional laws were being made illegally without any democratic process.

When I was in law school, I thought there was nothing meaningful that could be done to stop federal judges from illegally seizing law-making power. The only solution seemed to be that the President should appoint judges who would voluntarily choose not to exceed their power. My law professors rarely mentioned the problem and never talked about a solution.

Many years after graduating from law school, I assisted my oldest son in doing some research for a paper on the same subject. During that effort, I learned that there was a potential remedy for the problem in the U.S. Constitution, even though that constitutional remedy has never been used for that purpose in all of American history. I learned that some legal experts and members of Congress have proposed impeachment and removal for judges that exceed their power. Therefore, although the impeachment/removal issue has not been part of the mainstream of American politics, it has been raised.

I had been generally aware of the impeachment and removal provisions of the U.S. Constitution during law school. However, they were rarely discussed and never suggested as a way to stop judges who exceed their judicial power. Several years later, when I began thinking about writing this book, the impeachment/removal solution became a major theme.

A purpose of this book is to help make the illegal seizing of political power by judges part of the national political debate in America. Another purpose is to also make the only meaningful post-appointment constitutional check against that judicial practice, impeachment and removal of judges from office, a part of the national debate. I believe Americans should not sit by and let some members of the U.S. Supreme Court, and a few other judges, expand their judicial oligarchy.

A basic understanding of the relevant constitutional principles is necessary for a meaningful debate to take place. Those principles are explained below.

A Brief Summary Of The Issues Discussed In This Book

This section will provide a brief overview of the issues that are explained in detail in later chapters.

Over a period of more than half a century, the U.S. Supreme Court, and occasionally lower federal courts, have gradually but repeatedly created new constitutional law. They have done this by making what are in effect amendments to the U.S. Constitution, without the approval of the American people. This is contrary to the U.S. Constitution. The Constitution does not permit judges to make constitutional law and requires a "super majority" of votes by the elected representatives of the American people to amend the Constitution.

The provisions of the U.S. Constitution prevail over any other conflicting federal and state laws, even when "constitutional law" has been unconstitutionally created by federal judges. Therefore, in increasing areas of law governing American society, Americans are being ruled by unelected judges who are appointed for life-time tenures. U.S. Supreme Court justices and lower court judges are normally collectively referred to below as "judges."

The problems described above have placed America in danger of what Thomas Jefferson, the primary writer of the Declaration of Independence, feared from the federal judiciary almost 200 years ago: "[A] despotism of the oligarchy." [8] (An "oligarchy" is the governmental rule of a few people. "Despotism" essentially means dictatorship or tyranny).

One major consequence of these judicial practices is that the freedom of religious expression and other legal rights, which Americans have enjoyed for more than 200 years, are in jeopardy. Our constitutional rights are being significantly eroded by some federal judges that are exceeding their constitutional authority. These judges are negating the right to representative democracy of more than one hundred million voting-age Americans in the area of constitutional law.

The most commonly proposed solution to this practice of judicial law-making is for the President to appoint Supreme Court justices and other federal judges who will not engage in that judicial practice. Several Presidents have intended to do that only to find the appointed Supreme Court justices engage in judicial law-making, in spite of no past history of doing so. Once appointed, these judges are beyond that power of the President to remove them, or to otherwise influence their decision-making.

After a federal judge is appointed by the President, there is only one meaningful check in the U.S. Constitution on these practices of the federal courts. That check is the removal from office of federal judges by the U.S. Congress through impeachment procedures. Alexander Hamilton, a signer of the Constitution, called the constitutional procedures for impeachment and removal of judicial officers a "complete security" against law-making by federal judges. [9]

One purpose of this book is to cause Americans to demand that Congress seriously consider removing such judges from the bench, even though no federal judge has previously been removed from office for violating the U.S. Constitution by making law. Impeachment/removal procedures will be a "complete security" only if Congress fulfills its responsibility.

Most people who are against judicial law-making do not think impeachment and removal of federal judges is a politically likely remedy against judicial law-making. No federal judge has ever been removed from office for engaging in that practice in more than 200 years of American history, although efforts have arguably been made to do so. I believe that the likelihood of successfully impeaching and removing a Supreme Court justice from office is greater now than it has been in all of U.S. history. The reasons for that are discussed below.

Thomas Jefferson, James Madison and Alexander Hamilton will be quoted frequently in this book. The terms "framers" and "founders" will be used to refer to the people who were instrumental in developing the U.S. Constitution, including Jefferson, Madison and Hamilton. The writings of those framers of the Constitution are frequently quoted and relied upon by the U.S. Supreme Court in determining the meaning of the Constitution. For example, the U.S. Supreme Court sometimes quotes the *Federalist Papers*, a compilation of letters written to the American public mostly by Alexander Hamilton and James Madison. According to one political science writer, Thomas Jefferson said of the *Federalist Papers* that it is a document to which "appeal is habitually made by all, and rarely declined or denied by any" as to the "genuine meaning" of the Constitution. [10]

There are many examples of the courts effectively making constitutional law without approval of the American people. Compelled government recognition of same-sex marriage may become such an issue but has not yet reached the *federal* courts to a substantial enough degree. The right to abortion is also such an issue, but that subject is too complicated to address in this book.

The primary example of judicially-created constitutional law that will be discussed in this book is the "separation of church and state" doctrine. Although most of the current attacks on freedom of religious expression by the federal courts are against those of the Christian and Jewish faiths, the issues raised by this book transcend religious, philosophical, racial, and ethnic persuasion. Many of the rights of Americans, including the right to vote on amendments of the U.S. Constitutional, are under assault in the courts of our land. If the erosion of these constitutional rights continues, other rights Americans have enjoyed for more than 200 years are also in jeopardy.

The issues raised in this book also transcend political party affiliation and non-affiliation. Our constitutional rights are much more important than any political affiliation. I believe Americans should begin to vote based on conscience across party lines to require Congress to stop the courts from further eroding our constitutional rights.

Many Americans have died around the world defending the freedom and democratic ideals we enjoy. We should not stand by and let judicial officers dictate the laws imposed on us without firing a shot.

The Meaning Of The Title Of This Book

There is a dual meaning for the book title, *Walk Through The Wall, America.*

The term "WALL" refers metaphorically to the "wall of separation between church and state" discussed above. That "wall" is an illusion because it is not part of our nation's Constitution. I believe Americans should "walk through" that "wall" by demanding, among other things, that Congress remove from office those judges who expand the "separation of church and state" doctrine.

The term "WALL" also refers more generally to the wall of judge-made constitutional laws that deny the American people the right of self-government in the area of constitutional law. I believe Americans should also "walk through" that "wall" by requiring the President and Congress to take the appropriate actions regarding the federal judiciary.

A Brief Description Of Subsequent Chapters

Chapter Two provides a survey of the issues discussed in more detail in later chapters. Chapters Three through Five discuss the "separation of powers" and "federalism" doctrines in the U.S. Constitution. Those constitutional principles need to be understood in order to understand the other issues discussed in this book. The "separation of powers" doctrine relates to the division of federal governmental authority into three separate branches run by different people. The "federalism" doctrine relates to the apportionment of governmental power between the federal government and the state and local governments. Also discussed in Chapter Five are the democratic procedures for amending the Constitution.

Chapters Six through Nine relate to one area in which the federal judiciary has made an illegal constitutional amendment. As mentioned above, the example of judge-made law discussed here is the addition of the "separation of church and state" doctrine to the First Amendment by the U.S. Supreme Court in 1947. The most important chapters regarding the "separation of church and state" doctrine are Chapters Six and Seven.

Chapters Ten and Eleven explain the reasons and procedures for the impeachment/removal power, as well as the consequences and feasibility of impeachment and removal of federal judges. Chapter Twelve relates to the actions that can be taken by the American people to stop judicial tyranny.

If the reader wishes to have an overview, this chapter and Chapters Two, Ten, Eleven and Twelve should be read.

CHAPTER 2

A SURVEY OF JUDICIAL TYRANNY
AND WHAT CAN BE DONE ABOUT IT

The following simple hypothetical situation highlights the problem that is discussed in this book and summarized in this chapter: Suppose a nationwide initiative or referendum for a new constitutional amendment was put to a vote of the American people. Suppose further that a group of nine or fewer influential individuals hired tens of thousands of mercenaries and equipped them with guns. The mercenaries were then sent out to polling places to take, at gunpoint, ballots of Americans who came to vote on the referendum. The mercenaries proceeded to use the ballots to vote in a way that the influential individuals desired. If those influential individuals were government officials, should they be removed from office?

The foregoing hypothetical situation is similar in effect to what the United States Supreme Court has been doing for more than a half-century in some areas of constitutional law. Of course, the U.S. Supreme Court has not used violence or the threat of violence to change the U.S. Constitution. Instead, legal principles not found in the original or amended Constitution were put into it by the U.S.

Supreme Court. This has been repeatedly done by an anti-democratic process which is contrary to the Constitution.

If the threat of violence was used to take their right to vote away, the American people would be extremely angry. The American people would remove from power the perpetrators of such acts, if Americans had the power to remove them. However, the means used by the U.S. Supreme Court to change the U.S. Constitution has been no less effective than the threat of violence. It just took a longer period of time.

The Problem Of Judicial Tyranny

Most Americans believe that they should live under laws that are democratically determined. In other words, America's laws should be made by the elected representatives of the American people. If the American people are displeased about the laws their representatives enact, Americans can remove the representatives from office in the next election cycle. The newly-elected representatives can then change the undesirable laws. Most Americans believe that their laws should not be made by a small group of judges who are not voted into office, and can never be removed from office by an election process.

Unfortunately, this ideal of democracy, which many Americans believe should be theirs, does not exist in the area of constitutional law. By its own terms, the U.S. Constitution can only be changed by a "supermajority" vote of the elected representatives of the American people. However, for more than half of a century, the U.S. Constitution has been repeatedly changed by the votes of only five to nine Supreme Court justices. The votes of five to nine Supreme Court justices prevail in Supreme Court cases. Constitutional amendments have thus been made by these judges without any meaningful right of the American people to influence whether they want the U.S. Constitution to be altered.

Because they are determined to be part of the Constitution, these judicially-created constitutional amendments become the supreme law of the United States. Congress and the President cannot legally do anything that is contrary to constitutional laws. In other words, any laws passed by Congress (or by a state legislature) that are contrary to these judicially-created constitutional amendments are unconstitutional. Any unconstitutional laws are of no effect.

Some justices of the U.S. Supreme Court have effectively said that the political views of five to nine of them are more important than the votes of more than a hundred million Americans. About two hundred years ago, Thomas Jefferson predicted that the power of the U.S. Supreme Court to declare acts of Congress and the President unconstitutional "would place us under the despotism of an oligarchy." [1]

One leading commentator on constitutional law, Robert Bork, a former U.S. Court of Appeals Judge and Yale Law Professor, has recently stated the problem this way:

"Constitutional courts provide the necessary means to outflank majorities and nullify their votes. . . . Democracy and the rule of law are undermined while the culture is altered in ways the electorate would never choose." [2]

Bork went on the say that "the gradual replacement of democracy by judicial rule" threatens self-government and further stated as follows:

"At stake are personal freedoms. The fundamental freedom recognized in democracies is the right of the people to govern themselves." [3]

The Method Of Judicial Tyranny

The process used by the U.S. Supreme Court and some lower courts to change the Constitution has been repeated many times. Federal judges create a legal principle not in the Constitution that initially seems insignificant. Normally, the actual court decision with the new legal principle would cause most Americans who were aware of it to say, "so what?" or "I agree with that result." However, the legal principle created in the first judicial opinion is, in later cases, gradually expanded to construct a constitutional doctrine not in the Constitution itself. Decades later, that judicially-created doctrine is entrenched in the law as if it were written into the original Constitution, or into a constitutional amendment properly adopted by the only amendment process provided by the Constitution, a democratic process.

Today, judges and professors of law and political science are fond of quoting the writer of the Declaration of Independence and our nation's third President, Thomas Jefferson. Almost 200 years ago, Thomas Jefferson was very concerned about the tendency among judges, as he put it, "of going out of the question before them, to throw an anchor ahead and grapple further hold for future advances of [judicial] power." [4]

The method for creating illicit "advances of [judicial] power" that Thomas Jefferson was addressing is described above. That is what some federal courts, and especially the U.S. Supreme Court, have been doing in repeatedly changing the U.S. Constitution for more than half a century.

The Effect Of Judicial Tyranny

The effect of these judicially-created constitutional amendments is the same as a constitutional amendment that was approved under the carefully written democratic process provided by the Constitution. Who has done this? Federal judges who were appointed to usually life-time terms of office without any vote of the people. Furthermore, *these judges are never subject to removal from office by future elections*, as are the members of the U.S. Congress, or the U.S. Presidents.

Under present law, these illegal constitutional amendments cannot be changed unless the U.S. Supreme Court voluntarily decides to make a change, or an elaborate, lengthy process is followed to expressly correct unconstitutional amendments made by the Supreme Court. In other words, these anti-democratic, judicially-created laws are not only superior to all other laws, they are usually *permanent*, apart from a voluntary change of direction by the U.S. Supreme Court.

General Principles Of Constitutional Law Needed To Understand Judicial Tyranny

Before embarking on a discussion of an example of a judicially-created constitutional principle, the "separation of church and state" doctrine, this book will discuss some basic constitutional principles in Chapters Three through Five. These principles are the basis for the concepts that some judicial officers are acting outside of their constitutional authority, and should be considered for removal from office. This book will also address the basic procedures for amending the U.S. Constitution before turning to specific "separation of church and state" principles and decisions in Chapters Six through Nine. Finally, the constitutional reasons and principles for removing judges from office will be discussed in detail in Chapters Ten and Eleven. Chapter Twelve discusses what can practically be done by the reader.

For some readers, many of the basic constitutional principles may be known. In any event, it is not possible to understand the reasons for requiring Congress to exercise its power to impeach and remove judges, unless the basic principles are understood.

Summary Of The First Constitutional Protection Against Federal Tyranny: The Separation Of Powers Principle

To preview, federal judges have sometimes exceeded their constitutional authority because they have violated the fundamental "separation of powers" doctrine in our Constitution. The "separation of powers" doctrine is explained in more detail in Chapters Three and Four. By that doctrine, the American founders decided to divide the powers of government into different branches run by many different people. This was done in order to avoid the oppression they knew from Europe, where all governmental power was usually vested in one person, or a few people.

The founders chose to grant the general power to *make* laws to two groups of *elected* representatives, the House of Representatives and the Senate. Those representatives are collectively called the U.S. Congress. The Congress is the *legislative* branch of the federal government. [5]

The general power to *execute or enforce* the laws was given to the President, another elected official. This branch is called the *executive* branch. [6]

As discussed in more detail in Chapter Four, the general power to *apply* the law to specific disputes was given to the *judicial* branch. The judicial branch is made up of the U.S. Supreme Court and the lower courts. [7]

A judicial officer makes the decision when a "case" or "controversy" arises about how the Constitution, or other laws passed by Congress, applies to a particular situation.[8] Judicial officers are not elected by the people, but instead appointed to their positions by the President with the consent of the Senate.

As long as judges and justices stayed within their constitutional limits, the judicial branch was considered to be the weakest branch of the federal government. Judicial officers are thus appointed for indefinite, usually life-time terms. In other words, judicial officers are not voted into office by the American people, and are not subject to elections to remain in office. Federal judges almost always stay in office until they voluntarily leave office, or they die.

The judicial branch applies, among other things, the basic rights written into the original Constitution, and any amendments to the Constitution, to the facts of cases brought before it. Judicial officers do this by deciding specific disputes between individuals and/or organizations.

According to the Constitution, constitutional amendments can only be created by the *proposal* of two-thirds of the U.S. Congress (or two-thirds of the states), as well as the *ratification* of three-fourths of the individual States through their elected representatives. The procedures for amending the Constitution are discussed more thoroughly in the last section of Chapter Five.

Summary Of The Second Protection Against Federal Tyranny: The Federalism Principle

The federal government is further limited in its powers because of the constitutional doctrine of "federalism." Federalism is discussed in Chapter Five. The founders did not trust the concentration of all governmental power to make, enforce, and apply laws in the many people who would run the federal government. Therefore, all of the rights not specifically given to the federal government by the Constitution were expressly retained by the state governments and the American people.

The retention by the states and the American people of powers not expressly given to the federal government is set forth in the Tenth Amendment, which was ratified soon after the Constitution was ratified. That concept is also reflected in other provisions of the Constitution. However, the U.S. Supreme Court has substantially weakened this constitutional principle of federalism over the past 200 plus years, again without any democratically-ratified amendment. There is almost no government power that is left exclusively to the state governments, or the American people, today.

Another federalism principle is that federal law prevails over conflicting state law. Since constitutional law is the highest level of federal law, constitutional law created by the U.S. Supreme Court dominates all other conflicting laws in the United States, including laws enacted by Congress, as well as state and local governments.

The Inter-Branch Checks Against Federal Tyranny

As discussed more thoroughly in Chapters Three and Four, the powers of the federal government are also limited by specific checks and balances between the three branches. For example, the judicial branch has the power to declare laws enacted by Congress, or actions of the President, unconstitutional. Unconstitutional actions of Congress and the President are of no effect. This check on Congress and the President is not expressly stated in the Constitution, but was determined by the Supreme Court to exist in 1803.

The power of Congress and the President is also checked by the right of the American people to vote them into or out of office. There are other checks on both Congress and the President by the other governmental branches. Some of those checks are discussed below in Chapter Three.

Unlike the President and the Congress, if the U.S. Supreme Court does something that is unconstitutional, there is no other branch of the federal government to stop the U.S. Supreme Court. Thomas Jefferson summed it up this way:

"When the legislative [i.e., Congress] or executive [i.e., the President] functionaries act unconstitutionally, they are responsive to the people in their elective capacity. The exemption of judges from that is quite dangerous enough . . . . [The power of the judicial branch to declare acts of Congress and the President unconstitutional would be] very dangerous. . . [and] would place us under the despotism of an oligarchy." [9]

What Thomas Jefferson thought "would place us under the despotism of an oligarchy" is what has happened in our nation's constitutional law.

The Most Effective Solution To Judicial Tyranny

Many experts believe that the appropriate solution to prevent judicial law-making is for the President to appoint federal judges who will not exceed their power. That should work in theory. However, in practice, it has not worked. In recent decades, once appointed, most Supreme Court justices and some other federal judges have engaged in judicial law-making. This is true even though, in recent decades, most Supreme Court justices have been appointed by Presidents who intended to prevent that judicial practice.

There is only one meaningful check on the judicial branch by the other branches of government, after a federal judge takes office. That check is held by Congress. Congress has the power to impeach and convict federal judicial officers, thereby removing them from office.

Many people believe that the impeachment/removal power is not meaningful because Congress has not seriously considered that remedy to stop judicial law-making in the past. However, the political climate, both among the American people and in the Congress, is more conducive to that remedy now than ever before in U.S. history.

Another potential check on the federal courts is the power of Congress to reduce the extent of the federal courts' jurisdiction.[10] However, that would vest jurisdiction in the state courts, which would likely result in many or all of the same problems we have today. Other potential checks are also not currently feasible to stop judicial law-making.

One thesis of this book is that the American people should demand that Congress impeach and remove from office federal judges, and especially Supreme Court justices, who bypass the democratic process for amending the U.S. Constitution. The impeachment and removal issues are mentioned in Chapter Four, and are discussed in more detail in Chapters Ten and Eleven.

To summarize, the power to initiate a Congressional proceeding to remove federal judges is given to the House of Representatives. The power to conduct an impeachment trial and remove judicial officers resides in the Senate, by a two-thirds vote.

An impeachment and conviction of a federal judge by Congress, for exceeding the scope of his or her constitutional authority, could not be legitimately stopped. Congress has only very rarely used the impeachment/ removal power against federal judges, and has never used it to stop judicial law-making.

Removal of federal judges from office is not a drastic remedy but it would keep the removed judges from again abusing their judicial power. It may also deter some other judges from abusing their power in the future.

Alexander Hamilton called the impeachment/removal power of Congress a "complete security" against judicial law-making.[11] However, it is only a "complete security" if it is exercised by Congress.

Many judges and professors of law and political science are against any political process to remove judges for illegally engaging in law-making. Their reasoning is that judges protect constitutional and other individual rights and so should be "independent" of political removal. However, that assumes that judges stay within the bounds of their constitutionally granted power. When judges usurp power not given to them by making constitutional law, they should be subject to removal by the elected representatives of the American people. Otherwise, some judges may become dictators who are immune from accountability, thus fulfilling Jefferson's prediction of a "despotism of the oligarchy." [12]

Some people may be concerned about the unemployment, and the loss of the expertise, of judges who have given many years of public service. However, removal of judges would not harm America, or significantly harm the removed judges economically. There are many qualified people that can fill any vacancy in the federal courts. The removed judges would not go to jail and would probably be wealthier than they were as judges. They would probably be entitled to government pensions and have available to them many other lucrative income-producing opportunities. However, the removed judge would no longer be able to abuse his or her power.

Impeachment and removal are discussed in more detail in Chapter Five, and in Chapters Ten and Eleven.

A Minority Of Judges Have Engaged In Judicial Tyranny

It should be understood that this call for the removal of judicial officers would not be appropriate for most federal judges. Most judges simply apply existing precedential decisions of higher courts, which is their duty within our judicial system. Even though the laws they are applying may be unconstitutional, lower court judges are required to apply those laws if they were created by a court that is above them, such as the U.S. Supreme Court. On occasion, however, judges may *make new constitutional law* falsely claiming that they are following precedent.

Although many lower court judges may support the seizure of political power not given to the judicial branch by our Constitution, they usually do not usurp political power themselves. Such federal judges should not be removed from office.

On the other hand, as discussed throughout this book, some federal judicial officers have brazenly taken political power that is not theirs under the U.S. Constitution. They have abused their judicial power by imposing their personal views on other Americans. Such judicial officers should be seriously considered for removal from office.

I am not saying that these power-grabbing judges necessarily believe what they are doing is wrong or unlawful. These judges are applying the same process that has been employed by some of their predecessors, since before they began studying law. They are, however, making new constitutional law which did not exist for more than two centuries since the Constitution was ratified. The judicial career of a particular judge is far less important than preserving the right of the American people to govern themselves.

The Primary Example Of Judicial Tyranny Used In This Book: The "Separation Of Church And State" Doctrine

Many of the ideas expressed here can be applied to a wider, and continually increasing, wave of judicial decisions, which are effectively constitutional amendments. It is beyond the scope of this book to refer to them all.

Here, the focus will be on one judicially-created constitutional principle, the highly publicized "separation of church and state" doctrine. That doctrine is discussed in Chapters Six through Nine. This book will not, for example, discuss the broad "right of privacy" that was applied in the 2003 homosexual sodomy case mentioned in Chapter One (i.e., Lawrence v. Texas), and is also applied in abortion cases. The "right of privacy" in its broader form was created by judges. It is not in the Constitution. That issue, however, is too complicated to explain here.

To preview, the First Amendment is the ostensible basis for the "separation of church and state" doctrine. However, neither the First Amendment nor any other constitutional provision or amendment includes that language, or that concept. The only relevant language in the First Amendment states that "Congress shall make no law respecting an establishment of religion, or prohibiting the free exercise thereof . . . ."

The first ten words of the First Amendment stated above are called the "Establishment Clause." The remaining words are called the "Free Exercise" Clause. The Establishment and Free Exercise Clauses are collectively referred to as the "religion clauses."

In 1947, the U.S. Supreme Court added the "separation of church and state" concept to the Establishment Clause. However, "separation of church and state" is a much broader prohibitory concept than making no law respecting an *establishment* of religion. These issues are discussed thoroughly in Chapters Six and Seven.

What was the only basis for the "separation of church and state" doctrine? It was a phrase in a private letter written by Thomas Jefferson, in his capacity as a politician (i.e., the third President of the U.S.). This broadening of the First Amendment through a single politician's comment in a letter was a legally inappropriate means of determining the meaning of the U.S. Constitution.

The U.S. Supreme Court thus changed the First Amendment to suit the personal views of its members, without any democratic process whatsoever. As Thomas Jefferson himself put it, the U.S. Supreme Court threw "an anchor ahead" to grab "hold for future advances of [judicial] power," [13] when it created the "separation of church and state" doctrine.

In later cases, the U.S. Supreme Court has applied the

"separation of church and state" doctrine by creating a legal test for cases supposedly applying the First Amendment. As discussed below, this legal test is heavily biased in favor of non-theistic beliefs (i.e., belief systems excluding any relevance of a god). It has resulted in many decisions suppressing religious expression and history in public institutions.

The Voluntary Student-Led Prayer Cases

One type of "separation of church and state" decision relates to the exclusion of voluntary, student-initiated prayer and Bible study meetings in public schools. Those types of court cases are discussed in Chapter Eight. These cases violate, among others, the Supreme Court's First Amendment principle creating a free and open "marketplace of ideas." Although these cases were later effectively overruled by the U.S. Supreme Court, they illustrate the kind of unfair decision-making that the unconstitutional "separation of church and state" doctrine has spawned.

The religion clauses of the First Amendment have in some respects been determined to mean the opposite of their original meaning. For example, the Establishment Clause of the First Amendment originally meant, among other things, that *the federal government was required to stay away* from religious practices and expression in state-run public schools. Today, under the same language of the First Amendment, in conjunction with an alleged implied meaning of the Fourteenth Amendment, the Supreme Court has unconstitutionally determined that *the federal government is required to stop (through the federal judiciary)* most religious expression in state-run public schools. These issues are discussed in Chapter Six.

While I believe that religious instruction given *by public school officials* would be *very unwise* public policy, the actual Establishment Clause does not prohibit such a practice in state-run public schools. At most, the First

Amendment prohibits only the *federal government* from engaging in that practice. The U.S. Supreme Court has, however, determined that such a practice by a sate government is prohibited by making illegal amendments of the U.S. Constitution.

The U.S. Supreme Court should not have been permitted to change the Constitution without any democratic process whatsoever, as it has done through the "separation of church and state" doctrine, and by inappropriately applying the Establishment Clause to the states. Any laws prohibiting undesirable forms of religious expression in public schools should be made instead by democratically-elected legislative bodies, or by a democratically-ratified constitutional amendment.

The Ten Commandments Cases

Another kind of "separation of church and state" case is the exclusion of displays of the Ten Commandments from government facilities. These kinds of court cases, are discussed in Chapter Nine.

In excluding Ten Commandments displays from government facilities, the Supreme Court has required, among other things, a "secular purpose" for allowing such displays. The only Supreme Court case involving a Ten Commandments display found the display to be unconstitutional because it did not have a "secular purpose."

The Supreme Court has also determined that philosophical belief systems that do not have a faith in a god, such as atheism and *secular* humanism, are protected "religions" under the First Amendment religion clauses. The Supreme Court's "secular purpose" requirement thus favors non-theistic "religions," such as atheism and secular humanism.

The "secular purpose" requirement is not in the U.S. Constitution. The "secular purpose" requirement was derived from the "separation of church and state" doctrine.

As explained below, the U.S. Supreme Court has violated its purported stance of *"neutrality"* toward religious matters under the First Amendment. Chapter Nine discusses these issues in more detail.

More About This Book

This book is not designed to give the state of constitutional law in any particular area, including the "separation of church and state" doctrine. Nor is it the purpose to give a scholarly discussion of any legal issues. Instead, this book is written so that the American people are alerted to the threat to their freedoms that is posed by the federal judicial system, and to inform them what they can do about that threat.

CHAPTER 3

A DOCTRINE AGAINST FEDERAL TYRANNY: THE SEPARATION OF POWERS CONCERNING THE LEGISLATIVE AND EXECUTIVE BRANCHES

+≡≡+

Twelve-year old Johnny was still confused. His father was trying to explain the system of government to him. "So there are three branches?" Johnny ventured.

His father patiently answered, "Yes, the executive, legislative, and judicial branches. Before, the king had all the power of all three branches, which made it easy for him to do whatever he wanted. The king could put unfair burdens on the people and put his opponents in prison, or worse. There was no one who had the power to stop him or punish him when he became a bad king, a tyrant king. Now, the power is split up, so that won't happen anymore."

Johnny thought for a moment. "Why does splitting it up help?"

"Well, the legislative branch has the power to make the law, the executive branch makes sure that it's followed, and the judicial branch decides when people disagree about whether or not the law is being followed. When just one person or a small group has more than one of these powers, it is very difficult for others to stop the government from hurting people like the tyrant kings used to do. When different groups of people have these powers, the other branches can stop another branch from doing bad things."

"So what happens if a branch tries to be like a tyrant king?"

"Well, the legislative and executive branches have to be elected, so if we do not like what they are doing, we can just vote for someone else. The government officials who are elected know this, and so they rarely act like a tyrant king. Also, if the legislative branch makes a bad law, the executive branch can force the legislative branch to approve the law by a two-thirds vote. If the law is really bad, more than one-third of the people in the legislative branch will probably vote against it."

"What about that other branch? What happens if that one tries to act like a tyrant king?"

Johnny's father thoughtfully replied, "I am not certain. Perhaps I'll ask my lawyer friend."

Johnny started, "What if....?" But he broke off as he yawned and rubbed his eyes.

His father noticed and said, "It's getting late, son. You should get some sleep".

After tucking his son in for the night, he blew out the candle. Then he went into his study, sat at his desk, and dipped his quill into the inkwell to start a letter.

"Dear Alexander Hamilton ...."

About Chapters Three and Four

In order to understand why some judges have exceeded their authority, one must understand certain constitutional principles. The basic concepts in this chapter and Chapter Four are summarized in the sections of Chapter Two entitled

"Summary Of The First Protection Against Federal Tyranny-The Separation Of Powers Principle" and "The Inter-Branch Checks Against Federal Tyranny." If the reader wishes to skip further details regarding the "separation of powers" doctrine, including constitutional language and relevant principles articulated by some of the framers of the Constitution, the reader may turn to Chapter Five concerning the federalism doctrine and the procedures for amending the Constitution.

A copy of the relevant provisions of the U.S. Constitution and the first ten amendments to the Constitution, as well as the Fourteenth Amendment, are provided as Appendix A. The first ten constitutional amendments are collectively called the "Bill of Rights." In order to keep the federal government from becoming too powerful, the Bill of Rights was made a part of the Constitution soon after the original Constitution was ratified. The Eleventh through Twenty-Seventh amendments to the Constitution (with the sole exception of the Fourteenth Amendment) have not been provided because they are not relevant to the subjects discussed in this book.

The Constitution is actually elegantly simple for such a widely-applicable legal document. There are two main structural principles in the Constitution. They are called the "separation of powers" principle and the "federalism" principle. The separation of powers doctrine and some of its corollaries will be discussed in this chapter and Chapter Four.

The Nature And Purpose Of The Separation Of Powers Doctrine

The "separation of powers" refers to the division of federal governmental power among three branches. They are the legislative, executive, and judicial branches. Their principal provisions are found in Articles I, II and III of the Constitution, respectively.

In the Constitution, the founders separated the governmental powers because of the abuses of political power they knew from European history. The framers did not want all governmental power to be in the hands of too few people.

The division of the power of the federal government into different functions controlled by different groups of people was one of the two most important constitutional principles to the framers. Federalism was the other. For example, Thomas Jefferson's political philosophy on the separation of powers (as well as federalism) has been summarized as follows by David Mayer in his book, *The Constitutional Thought of Thomas Jefferson*:

> "Jefferson viewed constitutions primarily as devices by which governmental power would be limited and checked, to prevent its abuse through encroachment on individual rights (the Whig aspect of his thought). His preferred system for doing this was one in which governmental power was divided into distinct spheres (the federal aspect), each of which was in turn subdivided into *distinct branches (legislative, executive, and judicial)* equally accountable to the 'rightful' majority will of the people (the republican aspect)." [1]

James Madison, who is called by some the "Father of the Constitution," described the separation of powers this way:

> "*Power being found by universal experience liable to abuses*, a distribution of it into *separate departments*, has become a first principle of free governments. By this contrivance, the portion entrusted to the same hands being less, there is *less room to abuse what is granted*; and the different hands being

interested, each in maintaining its own, there is *less opportunity to usurp what is not granted.* Hence the merited praise of governments modeled on a partition of their powers into *legislative, executive, and judiciary,* and a repartition of the legislative into different houses." [2]

There are many other similar statements by these and other framers of the Constitution. The founders were strongly against putting political power in the hands of only a few people. They were aware of many oppressive governments that resulted from concentrated political power.

The U.S. Supreme Court itself has also emphasized the importance of the separation of powers principle as follows:

"We noted recently that '[t]he Constitution sought to *divide the delegated powers* of the new Federal Government into three defined categories, *Legislative, Executive, and Judicial. . .*' The declared purpose of separating and dividing the powers of government, of course, was to 'diffuse power' *the better to secure liberty.*

. . .

Even a cursory examination of the Constitution reveals the influence of Montesquieu's thesis that *checks and balances were the foundation of a structure of government that would protect liberty.*" [3]

Therefore, the separation of the federal government into three branches with different governmental powers is an extremely important protection of political freedom in America.

As discussed below, the legislative power is the power to legislate or make laws. The executive power is the power to execute or enforce the laws made by the legislature. The judicial power is the power to apply the laws made by the legislature to particular disputes between parties. The parties to such a dispute can be individuals, organizations including businesses, or governmental entities.

The Legislative Power: Law-Making

The basic legislative power is provided in Article I of the Constitution, which states:

> "All *legislative powers* herein shall be vested in a *Congress* of the United States, which shall consist of a *Senate* and a *House of Representatives*." **4**

The legislative branch is the only branch of the U.S. government which is given the power to make laws. Thus, only the U.S. Congress makes (i.e., legislates) the laws of the United States government.

There are other provisions in the Constitution which strongly suggest that only Congress can make laws, and can only do so in specific areas. For example, Article I, Section 8 specifically says "Congress shall have Power To…" and then lists seventeen specific areas in which Congress has the power to make laws. Congress does not have the power to make laws in areas not specifically listed in the Constitution.

The Tenth Amendment, which is discussed in Chapter Five, and the history behind its ratification, reiterates this principle. The other two branches, that is the executive and judicial branches, are given *no* power to make laws anywhere in the Constitution.

After listing seventeen specific powers to make laws given to Congress (i.e., the "enumerated powers"), Article I, Section 8 states that Congress shall have the power:

> "To *make all Laws* which shall be necessary and

proper for carrying into Execution the foregoing Powers, and all Powers vested by this Constitution in the Government of the United States." [5]

Thus, by this provision, Congress was given the power to make laws that were "necessary and proper" for carrying out the expressly stated powers. This "necessary and proper" clause was completely unnecessary if Congress was given the power to make any laws it desired to enact.

The language of the First Amendment also suggests that only Congress can make laws for the federal government. The First Amendment states:

> "*Congress shall make no law* respecting the estab-
> lishment of religion, or prohibiting the free exercise
> thereof... ." [6]

Why is only "Congress" mentioned in the First Amendment? Why does the first Amendment not say more broadly "The Government of the United States shall make no law..."? The reason is that the founders understood the Constitution to mean that no U.S. governmental body or officer other than Congress could make law.

There are many other reasons that law-making by the federal government is limited to Congress. The principle of limiting the law-making powers of the federal government to Congress has not been seriously challenged, in theory. However, that principle has been violated repeatedly by the U.S. Supreme Court, and occasionally the lower federal courts.

The Democratic Congressional Selection Process

The U.S. Congress is made up of the Senate and the House of Representatives. The Senate consists of two senators from each of the fifty states of the United States.

The House of Representatives is more representative of the population of the individual states than the Senate. The more populous states have more representatives, approximately in proportion to their population. Each representative is elected by the voters in a particular geographic subset of a state that contains a certain number of people.

Each Senator is elected to office and is subject to a reelection process every sixth year.[7] The members of the House of Representatives are also voted into office and subject to reelection every second year.[8]

Why are these details provided in this book about the judicial branch of the U.S. government? There are three reasons. First, only the U.S. Congress has the power to make the laws of the United States, not judges. Second, governmental power is spread out over many people. Third, those who make the laws of the U.S. are elected by the American people through a democratic process, and must be reelected to stay in office.

The Executive Power: Enforcing The Law

The basic executive power is provided in Article II, Section I of the Constitution which states:

> "The *executive power* shall be vested in a *President* of the United States of America. He shall hold his office during the *term of four years*, and together with the Vice President, chosen for the same term, be *elected ....*" [9]

Thus, the executive power is given to the President (or the Vice President if the President is unable to fulfill his duties). The President and Vice President are elected to office by an "electoral college" process, which was designed to generally reflect the aggregate votes of individual Americans, with a slight weighting in favor of the less-populated states. There is a new election for the President every four years. The President is limited to two four-year terms.

To fulfill his responsibilities, the President appoints cabinet members. The cabinet members direct various agencies which execute or enforce the laws made by the U.S. Congress. Examples of these agencies are the Department of Justice including the FBI (i.e., the Federal Bureau of Investigation which enforces federal criminal laws), the CIA (i.e., the Central Intelligence Agency, which watches foreign enemies of the U.S.), the military services, the EPA (i.e., the Environmental Protection Agency which implements environmental laws), etc. The President can remove the cabinet members if the President is displeased with their performance.

The Most Significant Checks On The Legislative And Executive Branches

Before addressing the judicial branch, some of the checks on the legislative and executive branches will be mentioned. The strongest check is the election process itself. If the American people are unhappy with the performance of a member of Congress or the President, they can vote that person out of office in the next election cycle.

Although not expressly found in the Constitution, another significant check on the legislative and executive branches is the power of the judicial branch (ultimately the U.S. Supreme Court) to declare a law enacted by Congress, or an action of the President, unconstitutional. If a law made by Congress, or an action of the President, is declared unconstitutional, it has no effect. This check was established by the U.S. Supreme Court in a legal case called <u>Marbury v. Madison</u> in 1803.[10]

There are other checks on the legislative and executive branches. For instance, the President may veto laws passed by a majority of both houses of Congress. On the other hand, the President's veto can be overridden by a vote of two-thirds of both the Senate and the House. The President's veto power and the veto override power of the Congress are found in Article I, Section 7.

Yet another check on the President's power is the ability of Congress to impeach him and remove him from office after a trial in the Senate. That check is found in Article II, Section 4.

CHAPTER 4

A DOCTRINE AGAINST FEDERAL TYRANNY: THE SEPARATION OF POWERS CONCERNING THE JUDICIAL BRANCH

Johnny's father tucked Johnny under the covers. "My lawyer friend, Alexander Hamilton, has responded to my letter about the tyrant king problem. Remember the other night when I told you about what can stop the executive and legislative branches from acting like a tyrant king, and you asked about what happens when the other branch acts like a tyrant king?"

"Oh, yeah! Now I remember," Johnny replied.

"Mr. Hamilton told me that we can't vote the people in the judicial branch, who are called judges, out of their positions. However, they can be removed from their positions by the legislative branch if they act like a tyrant king," explained Johnny's father.

"Does the legislative branch just kick judges out?" asked Johnny.

"No, it's not that simple. There are two groups in the legislative branch. The first group has to vote by more than half to make the second group do what's called a trial about a tyrant judge. After the trial, the second group must vote by two-thirds or more to remove the judge from his position."

Satisfied, Johnny closed his eyes and went to sleep.

About Chapter Four

The judicial branch of the federal government will be discussed in this chapter. The concepts discussed in this chapter were summarized in Chapter Two.

As explained below, the judicial branch has no power to make law. Instead, it decides disputes between parties by applying the law to the facts concerning a particular dispute. Judicial officers are not elected. They are appointed for potentially life-time terms. The other federal branches cannot declare an unconstitutional act of the U.S. Supreme Court of no effect. However, Congress can impeach and remove judges from office.

The Basic Federal Judicial Power

The basic judicial power is found in Article III, Section 1 of the Constitution which states:

> "The *judicial power* of the United States, shall be vested in one Supreme Court, and in such inferior courts as the Congress may from time to time ordain and establish. The judges, both of the supreme and inferior courts, shall hold their offices during good behavior..." [1]

Thus, the U.S. Supreme Court and any lower courts established by Congress exercise the judicial power. The U.S. Supreme Court has nine justices, one of which is designated as the Chief Justice. As mentioned above, the term "judges" in this book includes U.S. Supreme Court justices.

What is the "judicial power?" The judicial power is the power to apply the laws made by Congress, and the laws in the U.S. Constitution, to disputes between particular parties. The most relevant constitutional language is as follows:

> "The *judicial Power* shall extend to all *cases, in Law and Equity, arising under this Constitution, the Laws of the United States, and Treaties* made, or which shall be made, under their Authority…" [2]

Article III, Section 2 goes on to list some other specific, "cases" and "controversies" to which the judicial power extends. Thus, the judicial courts are only given the power to apply the law to specific disputes (i.e., "cases" and "controversies"). The courts, including the U.S. Supreme Court, are not given the power to make law by the U.S. Constitution.

The Structure Of The Judicial Branch

There are two levels of lower federal courts, the Courts of Appeals and the U.S. District Courts. All trials occur in the U.S. District Courts. That means that evidence such as the testimony of a witness can generally only be presented in the U.S. District Courts, the lowest level of the federal courts.

The first level of appeal of a decision by a U.S. District Court is to the U.S. Courts of Appeals. There are twelve Courts of Appeals. Eleven of them are cover various subsets of the fifty states. They are called the First through the Eleventh Circuit Courts of Appeals. The remaining Court of Appeals is for appeals in special legal cases such as patent cases. It is called the Court of Appeals for the Federal Circuit.

Parties have the *right* to appeal to the appropriate Court of Appeals. If an appeal from a Court of Appeals is available, it goes to the U.S. Supreme Court. With rare exceptions, the Supreme Court has discretion to refuse any appeal from the Courts of Appeals. Very few attempted appeals to the Supreme Court are accepted.

How Federal Judges Get Into And Stay In Office

U.S. Supreme Court justices, as well as lower court judges, are not elected or even approved by the American people. They are appointed by the President and confirmed by the Senate. To quote the Constitution, the President "nominate(s)" and "appoint(s)" judges "with the advice and consent of the Senate." [3]

The President cannot remove judges. Federal judges stay in office "during good [b]ehavior." [4] That means that federal judges are appointed for as long as they wish to stay in office, unless they are removed for some constitutional reason. Congress can remove judges through impeachment procedures discussed in briefly in this chapter and in more detail in Chapters Ten and Eleven.

It is very important who the President appoints to hold office in the U.S. Supreme Court and other federal courts. Many Presidents have tried to appoint Supreme Court justices who they thought would not engage in judicial law-making. However, once in office, many of these justices have engaged in that judicial practice even though they had not done so previously as lower federal or state judges.

Most Founders Thought The Judicial Branch Would Be Weak

Most of the founders thought that the judicial branch was the weakest branch of the three. For example, Alexander Hamilton argued that the "supposed danger of judiciary encroachments on the legislative authority" was "in reality a phantom" for the following reasons:

> "Particular *misconstructions and contraventions of the will of the legislature* may now and then happen; but they may never be so extensive as to amount to an inconvenience, or in any sensible degree to affect the order of the political system. This may be

inferred from *the general nature of the judicial power*, from the object to which it relates, from the manner in which it is exercised, from *its comparative weakness*, and from *its total incapacity to support its usurpations by force*." [5]

Hamilton's prediction that the federal judicial branch would never be an "inconvenience" to Congress, and that the judicial branch would never have much "affect on the order of the political system," was quite wrong. The extensive wrangling between the President and Congress over judicial appointments in recent years, and the many examples of the judicial branch making constitutional law, are among the current events that show how wrong Hamilton was about that issue. However, Hamilton's view was apparently shared by many of the other founders. The framers wrote more about their fears of usurpations of power by the legislative and executive branches, than they did about the judicial branch.

This belief in the weakness of the judicial branch is apparently one reason why there was only one substantial check on the judicial branch by the other branches of the federal government, after a judge is appointed to office. That check, impeachment and removal from office by Congress, is discussed below.

To summarize the main points about the judicial power, judges are not elected, or subject to future election. They were not given the power to make or enforce the law. Judges were only permitted to decide "cases" and "controversies" by applying the laws made by Congress and the American people. Thus, the Twentieth and Twenty-First Century practice of the judicial branch, primarily through the U.S. Supreme Court, of making constitutional law is not only anti-democratic, it is a violation of the U.S. Constitution.

There Is No Power To Void Unconstitutional Acts Of The Federal Judiciary

In the early years of the United States, there was debate about how determinations of constitutionality would be made by the branches of the federal government. The U.S. Constitution does not mention that issue.

Thomas Jefferson, who is often quoted by judges, law professors, and political scientists concerning the meaning of the original constitutional provisions and the Bill of Rights, believed that *each of the three branches should independently determine whether actions within its province was unconstitutional.* For example, he once stated as follows:

> "Our country has thought proper to distribute the powers of its government among three equal & independent authorities [i.e., branches], constituting each a check on one or both of the others, in all attempts to impair it's constitution. *To make each [branch] an effectual check*, it must have a right in cases which arise *within the line of it's proper functions*, where, *equally with the others*, it acts in the last resort & without appeal, *to decide on the validity of an act* according to it's own judgment, & *uncontrouled by the opinion of any other department.*" **6**

Thus, Thomas Jefferson believed that if Congress passed a law that the *President* thought was unconstitutional, the President could choose not to enforce it. If the *U.S. Supreme Court* also thought the law made by Congress was unconstitutional, the courts could refuse to apply the law to a controversy before them.

As another example, if the Supreme Court declared a law passed by Congress to be unconstitutional, the Congress and the President could ignore the Supreme Court if they disagreed. The Congress and the President would, however, have to answer to the American people in the next election cycle. If the American people agreed with the Supreme Court, they could remove the President and appropriate members of Congress from office by electing someone else.

Thomas Jefferson's views on determinations of constitutionality have *not* been adopted by the federal courts. At this time in our nation's laws, the federal courts have determined themselves to have the superior power to reach into the legislative and executive branches by declaring their actions unconstitutional and of no effect. This principle is generally believed to have been established in a U.S. Supreme Court case called <u>Marbury v. Madison</u>, (1803), when Thomas Jefferson was President.[7] That view of <u>Marbury v. Madison</u> has generally been practiced by the federal government since 1803.

President Andrew Jackson adopted Jefferson's view in the early 1830's when he rejected the U.S. Supreme Court's decision that Congress' recharter of the "Second Bank" was constitutional. President Jackson stated as follows in his veto of the recharter:

"The opinion of judges has no more authority over Congress than the opinion of Congress has over the judges, and on that point the President is independent of both." [8]

President Jackson's position is not generally considered to be correct today.

As explained above, there are theoretical constitutional limitations on what the judicial branch can do. The Supreme Court is theoretically prohibited from making constitutional law. However, *there is no current generally accepted means by which the actions of the U.S. Supreme Court can be declared unconstitutional by any other branch.* Thus, there is no way to stop the U.S. Supreme Court from illegally making constitutional law. In other words, the separation of powers limitation which prevents the courts from making constitutional law is effective only as long as judges voluntarily stay within their limited powers.

The Only Meaningful Post-Appointment Check On The U.S. Supreme Court: Impeachment And Removal By Congress

Since the President appoints federal judges into office, the President can theoretically prevent judges from exceeding their power by appointing judges who will voluntarily avoid judicial law-making (assuming the Senate confirms such appointments by the President). In practice, however, this idea has frequently not been successful. During the last several decades, Presidents have appointed most Supreme Court justices believing those judges would not exceed their judicial power.

Once appointed, however, most of those judges have repeatedly engaged in judicial law-making. After appointment, there was nothing these Presidents could do to stop these judges.

There is another remedy in the Constitution if the judicial branch exceeds its power. That remedy is impeachment and removal of judges from office by Congress. In the *Federalist Papers*, Alexander Hamilton called impeachment procedures a "complete security" against "judiciary encroachments on the legislative authority." [9]

Making constitutional amendments is dependent on the "legislative authority" because both Congress and the state legislatures have the key roles in that process, as discussed in Chapter 5. Therefore, the creation of constitutional amendments by the judiciary is an "encroachment [] on the legislative authority" about which Hamilton said impeachment procedures were the "complete security." [10]

The impeachment/removal check on the judicial branch is discussed briefly here, and in more detail in Chapters Ten and Eleven. No U.S. Supreme Court justice has ever been removed from office in more than 200 years of U.S. history. Only one Supreme Court justice was impeached by the House, but the Senate voted not to remove him in 1805. His name was Samuel P. Chase.

Only about a dozen federal judges at any court level have been impeached, and fewer have been convicted and removed, in more than two centuries since the Constitution was ratified. No federal judge has been removed from office for exceeding the judicial power by engaging in law-making.

There is another potential check on U.S. District Court judges *within the federal judicial system.* The decisions of U.S. District Court judges can be appealed to a Court of Appeals as a matter of right. Court of Appeals decisions are, in rare cases, taken on appeal by the U.S. Supreme Court. However, *there is no appeal of the decisions of the U.S. Supreme Court.*

The other branches of the federal government can theoretically exercise other checks on the federal courts but those checks are not very meaningful at this juncture in our nation's history. For example, under Article III, Section 2, *Congress can limit the jurisdiction of the federal courts to decide cases.* [11] This would, however, throw jurisdiction by default to the state courts which in most instances are as likely to engage in law-making as the federal courts. In some instances, state courts are more likely to engage in law-making than the federal courts.

Congress could pressure the federal courts by denying the funding they need to function, or by placing heavy legal burdens on the courts. That would severely damage the economy, however, because the resolution of business disputes, including the protection of fair competition, would nearly come to a halt. Congress is, therefore, highly unlikely to do that.

The number of Supreme Court justices could be increased by Congress, thus allowing the President to appoint more justices. President Franklin D. Roosevelt tried to do that during the 1940's, and failed. That approach is highly improbable and does nothing to deter or stop the old or new justices from engaging in law-making.

Needless to say, U.S. Supreme Court justices are very powerful people in our federal government. They are not subject to approval or removal by the American people through elections of federal judges. The responsibility to exercise the only meaningful check after Presidential appointment of federal judges, impeachment and removal, is left to Congress. Removal requires a two-thirds majority in the Senate, after a trial.

The Rationales For Having Only A Single Meaningful Check On The Judiciary

Why did the founders establish judicial offices with no power to reelect or reject the office holders? The answer in part was that the founders thought the judiciary was weak and so elections were unnecessary. The judicial branch could not make or enforce the law. Judges did not control the U.S. government's taxing and spending power, the military or the federal police force. They supposedly only had power to determine how the laws made by Congress, or the laws in the Constitution, were to be applied to particular disputes.

There is another rationale for the unelected status of the judicial branch. Judges are not subject to elections because they should remain "independent" of political pressure. The judiciary is supposed to protect the democratically-ratified constitutional rights of minority groups and individuals who are not in the majority of voters on a particular issue.

The independence of federal judges in protecting demo-cratically-created constitutional rights of individuals and minorities is very important. However, what happens when federal judges (and especially U.S. Supreme Court justices) exceed their power and make *new constitutional rights*, or *destroy existing constitutional rights*, without any vote by Congress or the American people? There should be no "independence" for judges who engage in that illegal practice. Any action of an unelected governmental body such as the U.S. Supreme Court to make new laws is dictatorship, not democracy. That issue is especially important in constitutional law, the supreme law of the United States.

When judges make law they are injecting themselves into the political process of law-making. When judges do that they *should* receive political pressure. In other words, the votes of the American people should be able to influence the decisions of judges who engage in law-making. Impeachment and removal of federal judges by Congress is the only meaningful way to bring such pressure to bear.

ANOTHER PROTECTION AGAINST FEDERAL TYRANNY: THE DOCTRINE OF FEDERALISM; AND THE ONLY PROCEDURES FOR AMENDING THE CONSTITUTION

The second major principle in the U.S. Constitution, other than the separation of powers, is "federalism." The concepts in this chapter are summarized in the sections of Chapter Two entitled "The Problem of Judicial Tyranny" (second and third paragraphs) and "Summary Of The Second Protection Against Federal Tyranny—The Federalism Principle" (as well as the paragraph immediately preceding that section of Chapter Two). If the reader wishes to skip the additional details about those issues, the reader may turn to Chapter Six which begins the discussion of the "separation of church and state" doctrine.

Introduction To Federalism

The federalism principle relates to the division of power between the federal or U.S. government, and the governments of the fifty individual states. When the U.S. Constitution was enacted, the states were forming a federation to create a limited centralized government. The original thirteen states had prior histories as separate colonial governments. When independence from Britain was achieved, the states (e.g., Massachusetts, New York, Pennsylvania, Virginia, North Carolina, Georgia, etc.) were essentially separate countries with geographic proximity.

The concept of federalism is discussed in this book in order to show that the federal government was supposed to be limited in its power to make laws. The new federal government was not intended by the founders to be able to make whatever laws federal officials desired.

The federalism doctrine is also explained to show that the laws of the U.S. Constitution are superior to all other laws in America. Therefore, it is extremely important what the U.S. Supreme Court and other judicial courts say is in the U.S. Constitution.

The difficult procedure by which the U.S. Constitution can be changed is also discussed in this chapter. Constitutional law cannot be changed other than by a lengthy democratic process, or illegally by a decision of the U.S. Supreme Court.

The Limited "Enumerated Powers" Of
The Federal Government

The individual states did not want to give up their right to govern themselves when the U.S. Constitution was ratified. All of the signatories to the U.S. Constitution were representatives of particular states that had independent prior histories. The states thus limited the new federal government to certain "enumerated powers" to make federal laws.[1] These enumerated federal law-making powers were discussed in Chapter Three. All other rights to make laws were reserved to the American people through their state and local governments. [2]

These federalism concepts are clear from the express terms of the U.S. Constitution and the Bill of Rights (i.e., the first ten constitutional amendments), as well as the history of those constitutional provisions. The Bill of Rights was ratified soon after the Constitution because most of the framers were concerned that the federal government would encroach on the rights of the states and the people to govern themselves. The federalism principle was intended as a significant check against an overly powerful federal government.

Thomas Jefferson expressed the importance of the federalism concept as follows:

> *"[W]hen all government*, domestic and foreign, in little as in great things, *shall be drawn to Washington* as the center of all power, it will *render powerless the checks provided of one government on another*, and will become as venal and oppressive as the government from which we separated. It will be as in Europe, where every man must be either pike or grudgeon, hammer or anvil." [3]

As explained in the foregoing chapters on the separation of powers, only the U.S. Congress was given the power to make laws for the federal government. The "enumerated powers" to which the U.S. Congress was limited are contained in Article I, Section 8 of the Constitution. In spite of this, the power of the federal government to make law has been expanded by the federal courts substantially beyond that contemplated by the founders, without any constitutional amendments being ratified.

The Tenth Amendment's Reservation Of Governmental Powers To The States And To The People

All governmental power to make laws not specifically given to the federal government by the Constitution was exclusively reserved to the states and the American people by the Tenth Amendment, which says:

> *"The powers not delegated* to the United States by the Constitution, nor prohibited by it to the States, are *reserved to the States* respectively, or *to the people."* [4]

The Tenth Amendment is part of the "Bill of Rights" which was ratified soon after the original Constitution. When the U.S. Constitution and the Bill of Rights were being debated and negotiated, those who opposed the Bill of Rights argued that the Bill of Rights was unnecessary. In other words, some framers argued that since the federal government was limited to the powers specifically set forth in the Constitution, there was no need to have a Bill of Rights setting forth rights that were retained by the people or the states.

The Bill of Rights (including the Tenth Amendment quoted above) was ratified in spite of those arguments. Most of the framers simply did not trust the federal government to voluntarily stay within its bounds. They were correct. The federal government has not stayed within its limitations, in spite of the Bill of Rights.

Over the last more than two centuries since the Bill of Rights was ratified, the Tenth Amendment's concept of powers being exclusively reserved to the states and the people has gradually been rendered almost meaningless by encroachments of the federal government, with the approval of the federal courts. Most of those encroachments occurred during the Twentieth Century, more than one hundred years after the federal courts were established.

Thomas Jefferson anticipated the encroachment of the federal courts on the governmental powers retained by the states and the people:

"[The federal judiciary is] an *irresponsible body. . .* working like gravity by night and by day, *gaining a little to-day and little to-morrow*, and *advancing its noiseless step like a thief*, over the field of jurisdiction, until *all shall be usurped from the States*, and the government be consolidated into one." [5]

Jefferson had no confidence that judges (or any other persons) who were employed by the federal government would voluntarily respect the limits that the Constitution placed on them. He described the "espirit de corps" of the judiciary as including the idea that "it is the office of a good judge to enlarge its jurisdiction." [6] He simply did not trust people with unchecked governmental power, no matter how strong their character, because of the inherent susceptibility of human beings to give in to the lust for power. [7]

Regarding the division of power between the federal and state governments and the strong tendency of the federal courts to favor the federal government, Jefferson said:

"[H]ow can we expect impartial decision between the General government, of which they [federal judges] are themselves so eminent a part, and an individual state from which they have nothing to hope or fear." [8]

To summarize, because of repeated encroachments permitted and made by the U.S. Supreme Court, today there are few, if any, powers that are "not delegated" to the federal government and "reserved" to the states, or the American people. The Tenth Amendment has been considerably weakened under the jurisdiction of the U.S. Supreme Court.

The Supremacy Clause
There is one other very important concept of federalism

which is relevant to this book. That concept is that the laws of the federal government are superior to the laws of the state governments. That principle is found in the "Supremacy Clause" of Article VI, Clause 2, which states:

"This *Constitution*, and the *Laws of the United States which shall be made in pursuance thereof*; and all Treaties made, or which shall be made, under the Authority of the United States, *shall be the supreme Law* of the Land; and the Judges in every State shall be bound thereby, *any Thing in the Constitution or Laws of any State to the Contrary notwithstanding*." [9]

Thus the laws of the federal government are superior to the laws of the states. Moreover, the U.S. Constitution is superior to all other laws, including those enacted by Congress.

In view of the foregoing principles, if the U.S. Supreme Court determines that a law is "found" in the U.S. Constitution (whether or not the U.S. Supreme Court's determination is correct), the only way to change the judicially-created constitutional law is to go through an elaborate, lengthy procedure to amend the U.S. Constitution.[10] Neither Congress alone, nor any state government, can change any such constitutional "law" created by the U.S. Supreme Court, even if the Supreme Court's judge-made law is unconstitutional. Because the newly created "law" is in the Constitution according to the U.S. Supreme Court, it is presently the "supreme" law of the United States.

In other words, if the Congress or a state legislature enacts a law contrary to any legal principle "found" in the Constitution by the U.S. Supreme Court, the U.S. Supreme Court will eliminate that law by declaring it to be unconstitutional.

Furthermore, if one state more than *one-quarter* of the states agrees with the U.S. Supreme Court, any illegal judge-made amendment by the U.S. Supreme Court *cannot* be corrected. The people of America should not be required to go through such a process to correct an illegal seizure of power by the U.S. Supreme Court.

The Only Constitutional Mechanism For Amending The U.S. Constitution: A Democratic Process

The procedure for amending the U.S. Constitution was designed to be very difficult. It is found in Article V of the Constitution.

In order to propose a particular amendment to the U.S. Constitution, two-thirds of the members of both houses of Congress, or the legislatures of two-thirds of the states, must vote for the amendment. However, that is only necessary, not sufficient.

For an amendment to be ratified, there also must be approval by three-fourths of the legislatures of the fifty states. Alternatively, conventions of elected officials in three-fourths of the fifty states may ratify the amendment.

The relevant constitutional provision provides as follows:

"The Congress, whenever *two thirds of both Houses* shall deem it necessary, shall propose Amendments to this Constitution, or, on the Application of the *Legislatures of two thirds of the several States*, shall call a Convention for proposing Amendments, which, in either Case, shall be valid to all Intents and Purposes, as part of this Constitution, when *ratified by* the Legislatures of *three fourths of the several States*, or by Conventions in three fourths thereof, as the one or the other Mode of Ratification may be proposed by the Congress . . . ." [11]

In view of the foregoing, it is very difficult to ratify a constitutional amendment. Only seventeen express amendments (the Eleventh Through Twenty-Seventh Amendments) have been ratified during the more than two centuries since the Constitution and the Bill of Rights were ratified. However, the U.S. Supreme Court has repeatedly amended the Constitution through incremental changes that, over a period of decades, have resulted in huge changes in the U.S. Constitution.

CHAPTER 6

AN INTRODUCTION TO THE "SEPARATION OF CHURCH AND STATE" DOCTRINE, AN EXAMPLE OF JUDICIAL TYRANNY BY FEDERAL JUDGES

What is an example of judicial law-making by federal judges? This chapter and Chapters Seven through Nine discuss one such example. A hypothetical story related to most of the issues raised in this chapter is provided in the "Prologue" immediately before Chapter One.

A constitutional principle called the "separation of church and state" was illegally put into the First Amendment of the U.S. Constitution by the U.S. Supreme Court in 1947. That language is not found anywhere in the U.S. Constitution or the Bill of Rights, including the First Amendment.

The First Amendment provides in relevant part as follows:

"Congress shall make no law respecting an establishment of religion, or prohibiting the free exercise

thereof, or abridging the freedom of speech ...." [1]

The First Amendment provides that "Congress shall make no law respecting an establishment of religion . . . ," not that there is a "separation of church and state." By way of reminder, the first ten words set forth above are called the "Establishment Clause." The following five words are called the "Free Exercise Clause." The remaining words are called the "Free Speech Clause," or are generally referred to as the "freedom of speech."

The "Separation of Church and State" Concept Is A Broader Prohibition Than The Establishment Clause

The "separation of church and state" doctrine was created in a case called <u>Everson v. Board of Education</u> (1947). [2] That doctrine is supposedly based on the Establishment Clause of the First Amendment. As is discussed below, the "separation of church and state" doctrine has been used to stop many actions by state and local governments, such as those in public schools.

The Bill of Rights, which includes the First Amendment, was ratified soon after the rest of the Constitution was adopted. *The purpose of the Bill of Rights was to prevent the new federal government from interfering with the basic rights enjoyed by the people of America, including those already established in the laws and practices of the state governments.* Those who opposed the Bill of Rights argued that the first ten amendments were unnecessary because the federal government was limited to the powers enumerated in the main body of the Constitution. In spite of that argument, the states ratified the Bill of Rights because the American people did not trust people who possess governmental power.

The judge-made "separation of church and state" doctrine is a much broader and stronger prohibition than the actual language of the Establishment Clause. As discussed in Chapter One, the Second Circuit Court of Appeals in Brandon v. Guilderland Board of Education (1980) stated that if the "separation of church and state" principle was "strictly" applied, religious institutions such as parochial schools and churches would not receive police and fire protection from the government.[3] In applying the "separation of church and state" doctrine to prohibit a student club from engaging in voluntary, student-led prayer in a public school, the Brandon Court put it this way:

> "A *strict reading* of the Establishment Clause's erection of the Wall between church and state would require government to refrain from providing even the most *essential public services* to religious organizations. Such *inflexible separation*, however, threatens free exercise, and therefore the principle of neutrality requires the state to provide *fire and police services*. . . to religious schools and organizations. . . . Accommodation of these three constitutional values is a trying task, but one in which courts are compelled to engage. [4]

In other words, people could burn down churches, synagogues and religious schools and kill their occupants without any intervention by the fire or police departments, if the "separation of church and state" doctrine was "strictly" or "inflexibly" applied! The Establishment Clause itself could not reasonably lead to that result even if it was "strictly" applied in isolation from other provisions of the First Amendment. Therefore, the "separation of church and state" doctrine is a much stronger prohibition than the actual language of Establishment Clause.

The Establishment Clause Prohibited Only Actions By The Federal Government, Not The State Governments, When It Was Enacted

The actual language of the Establishment Clause prohibits *only Congress* from making any law "respecting an establishment of religion" before 1947. Since Congress is the only governmental branch that was permitted to make law under the Constitution, the Establishment Clause effectively prohibits the entire federal government from making such laws. The state governments are not prohibited from doing anything by the actual language of the Establishment Clause.

That the purpose of the Establishment Clause was to prohibit only the federal government from making laws regarding an establishment of religion, not the state governments, is not only supported by the language of the First Amendment. It is also supported by the historical context of the First Amendment and the proceedings in Congress that resulted in the Establishment Clause.

When the First Amendment was ratified, at least *five of the states had state-sponsored establishments (i.e., denominations) of religion.* Among those states were Massachusetts, New Hampshire, Connecticut, Maryland and South Carolina. [5]

Furthermore, during the early years of the United States religion was taught in the state governments' public schools by public school officials. As fairly recently stated in 2002, by three U.S. Supreme Court Justices:

"[H]istorians point out that during the early years of the Republic, American schools-including the first public schools-were Protestant in character. Their students recited prayers, read the King James version of the Bible, and learned Protestant religious ideals." [6]

Thus, in view of the language of the First Amendment and its historical context, it is clear that *the state and local governments were not prohibited from making laws respecting an establishment of religion and respecting mandatory religious practices*, after the First Amendment was in place. The state governments already had "establishments" of religion and continued to have religious establishments after the First Amendment was ratified.

How did the First Amendment in the Bill of Rights, which was designed in part to keep the federal government from interfering with the religious practices of state governments, become the vehicle for prohibiting state and local government (e.g., public schools) from engaging in *any* practice, especially practices that were commonplace when the First Amendment was adopted? That will be explained below. In short, it was done illegally by the U.S. Supreme Court.

The most important point is that *the people of America and their elected representatives had no right to vote* on the "separation of church and state" doctrine, or on the application of the First Amendment to the states, which were both imposed in the 1947 <u>Everson</u> case. Instead, unelected federal judges unconstitutionally put the "separation of church and state" concept into the First Amendment, and unconstitutionally applied it to the states. The U.S. Supreme Court did this by exercising power which was withheld from judges by the Constitution.

The First Amendment Free Exercise Clause And The "Separation Of Church And State" Principle

As discussed in the first section of this chapter, the concept of "separation of church and state" is much broader than the concept of no law regarding an "establishment of religion." The actual language of the Establishment Clause prevents the U.S. Congress from establishing a federally-approved religious denomination, or requiring people to engage in religious practices. It may also prohibit Congress from funding only the religious activities of a religious denomination. However, the Establishment Clause itself does not prohibit government funding of the activities of non-religious and religious organizations alike.

The actual Establishment Clause also does not prohibit voluntary religious *expression* in governmental institutions. It prohibits a federal law respecting an *establishment* of religion, not respecting religious *expression*. There were many examples of religious expression by the federal government before and after the First Amendment was ratified. For example, the members of Congress who wished to do so have always opened each session of Congress by participating in spoken prayer. Congress has done this since the founding of the United States, and still does it today. The decisions and arguments against religious expression in government institutions are based on the much broader "separation of church and state" doctrine, which is *not* in the First Amendment.

What other language *is* in the First Amendment? The First Amendment says that "Congress shall make no law… prohibiting the free exercise" of religion. This language is called the "Free Exercise Clause." The Free Exercise Clause is in the same sentence of the First Amendment as the Establishment Clause. Thus, *the only language in the First Amendment that expressly addresses the issue supports freedom of religious expression*, in governmental institutions or otherwise.

In spite of the express language protecting the "free exercise" of religion from being limited by the federal government, religious expression has been repeatedly prohibited by the U.S. Supreme Court since 1947. This has happened because the "separation of church and state" doctrine was illegally added to the First Amendment by the U.S. Supreme Court without any democratic process, in the Everson case.

The "separation of church and state" doctrine (which is *not* in the First Amendment) usually dominates the free exercise clause (which *is* in the First Amendment). That is to say nothing about the freedom of speech, which is also expressly provided in the First Amendment, unlike the "separation of church and state" doctrine.

The Application Of The First Amendment To The States By "Implication" Through The Fourteenth Amendment Was Unconstitutional

In the <u>Everson</u> case, the U.S. Supreme Court illegally reversed the First Amendment religion clauses from a *protection* of state government religious practices and laws for more than 150 years, to a *prohibition* of many of the same practices and laws after 1947.

As mentioned above, the religion clauses refer to "Congress" because Congress is the only branch of the federal government that is authorized to make law. Therefore, the language of the Establishment Clause and the Free Exercise Clause *prohibits only the federal government* from making a law regarding an "establishment of religion," or prohibiting the "free exercise" of religion. There is no restriction on the states in the language of the First Amendment.

In spite of the foregoing, the religion clauses have been repeatedly applied to *stop the actions of state and local governments*. How has the federal judiciary done this? The U.S. Supreme Court has forced the religion clauses on state and local governments *by implying* that the Fourteenth Amendment required them to do so.

What does the Fourteenth Amendment actually provide? The relevant part of the Fourteenth Amendment provides:

"No State shall make or enforce any law which shall abridge the privileges and immunities of citizens of

71

the United States; *nor shall any State deprive any person of life, liberty, or property, without due process of law*; nor deny to any person within its jurisdiction the equal protection of its laws." [7]

The above italicized language from the Fourteenth Amendment is called the "due process clause." In Cantwell v. Connecticut (1940), the Supreme Court held that the Fourteenth Amendment "due process" clause *impliedly* applied the Free Exercise Clause to the states. [8] In Everson v. Board of Education (1947), the same result was *implied* regarding the Establishment Clause. [9] *Those cases "found" those implications with no explanation other than generally referring to the "liberty" portion of the due process clause.*

The implications "found" by the Supreme Court are simply not in the language of the Fourteenth Amendment. The "due process" clause relates to the appropriate legal *processes* to be used to protect "life, liberty or property," *not* to the *substantive liberties* in the First Amendment or elsewhere. An example of a legal "process" would be a hearing before a judge in which witnesses can testify, as opposed to an arbitrary decision by a government bureaucrat, without a hearing or the testimony of witnesses.

In the law, legal "process" (i.e., legal procedure) is conceptually separate from "substantive law." The rights set forth in the First Amendment are "substantive law." Therefore, based on traditional legal analysis, the extent or application of the "substantive" rights in the First Amendment, including those set forth in the religion clauses, are not determined by the "procedural" provision in the Fourteenth Amendment's due process clause. However, the Supreme Court has declared otherwise.

The *Fifth* Amendment in the original Bill of Rights expressly applied the same "due process" clause *to the federal government* that is applied to the states in the

Fourteenth Amendment.[10] Therefore, the Fourteenth Amendment simply required the states to adhere to the same "due process" principles (i.e., procedural principles) that the Fifth Amendment required the federal government to adhere to. The *Fourteenth* Amendment does not imply application of the First Amendment to the states any more than the *Fifth* Amendment implies application of the First Amendment to the federal government. Instead, the *First* Amendment applies to the federal government, and *only* the federal government, *by its own terms.*

The Supreme Court's Fourteenth Amendment "implication theory" is especially inappropriate regarding the Establishment Clause. As explained above, a major effect of the Establishment Clause *before* the Fourteenth Amendment was ratified in 1868, was to prevent the federal government from interfering with the religious practices of the state governments and the people. Thus, a primary *"liberty" interest that was protected by the Establishment Clause* was collectively owned by the people of each particular state. That "liberty" interest *allowed the people, through their state government democratic laws, to determine the proper interface between the state governments and religion.*

In spite of the foregoing, the <u>Everson</u> case created a law that implements the *opposite* of that "liberty" interest in the Establishment Clause. After the <u>Everson</u> case, the federal government is supposedly required to interfere with most religious practices of state governments through the Fourteenth Amendment implication theory. Thus, the above-described "liberty" interest in the Establishment Clause was not merely applied to the states in the <u>Everson</u> case. That "liberty" interest was instead destroyed.

Other Reasons That The First Amendment Establishment Clause And The Free Exercise Clause Are Not Applicable By "Implication" To State Governments

There is another problem with the effect of the Fourteenth Amendment implication theory, assuming for the sake of argument that the "implication" exists. As mentioned above, the First Amendment religion clauses prohibit "Congress" from making a law regarding an establishment of religion, or prohibiting the free exercise of religion. There is, and never has been, a "Congress" in any of the states. Therefore, even if the religion clauses were impliedly applied to the states by the Fourteenth Amendment (and they were not), they have no effect against the state governments.

In addition, Congress *rejected* proposed constitutional amendments which would have applied the religion clauses to the states in both 1875 and 1937, after the Fourteenth Amendment was ratified in 1868. The second failed attempt occurred only three years before the Supreme Court imposed the Free Exercise Clause by judicial edict in the Cantwell case, in 1940. [11]

The first proposed constitutional amendment requiring the states to adhere to the religion clauses was proposed by Senator James Blaine in 1875, and read in part as follows:

> "No State shall make any law respecting an establishment of religion or prohibiting the free exercise thereof . . ." [12]

As mentioned above, this proposed amendment was rejected by Congress and so was never ratified. A similar amendment was proposed in 1937, and again rejected. [13]

The Fourteenth Amendment was ratified in 1868. If the Fourteenth Amendment applied both of the religion clauses to the states by "implication" in 1868, as the <u>Everson</u> Court said, why did some members of Congress try unsuccessfully to do so expressly through Article V's difficult amendment process in both 1875 ad 1937? Also, why did it take the nation more than 70 years to "discover" the supposed implication that was imposed in the <u>Everson</u> case by the U.S. Supreme Court? The response to both questions is that there was no such implication. The Supreme Court applied the "implication theory" to the Establishment Clause almost 80 years after the Fourteenth Amendment was ratified because it wanted a certain result, not because the "implication" was actually present in the Fourteenth Amendment.

In fact, when the Blaine Amendment was proposed in 1875, the Congressional debates indicated that the intent of the Fourteenth Amendment was *not* to apply the First Amendment to the states. [14] That is the kind of information the federal courts often rely on in deciding these kinds of issues. The U.S. Supreme Court did not analyze or even mention the foregoing facts in the <u>Everson</u> case.

If Congress and the states that ratified the Fourteenth Amendment intended that the Fourteenth Amendment caused the "substantive" provisions in the First Amendment's religion clauses to be applied to the states, they would have made it reasonably clear in the language of the Fourteenth Amendment. That is especially true regarding the Establishment Clause because a substantial part of the meaning of that clause would be *reversed* by applying it to the states. Congress and the states did not make such a change of meaning reasonably clear. The Supreme Court's decisions to create that result were thus unconstitutional.

The U.S. Supreme Court illegally did what Congress rejected because the Supreme Court's members desired that result, and because they believed correctly that they could do so without any penalty. That is a form of dictatorship, not democracy.

Even If Some Establishment Clause Principles Are Desirable, That Does Not Justify The Supreme Court Exceeding Its Power, As The Supreme Court Itself Has Suggested

Neither I, nor even a significant minority of Americans, advocate state-sponsored religious denominations or mandatory religious instruction *by public school officials* today. Therefore, if the "separation of church and state" doctrine is eliminated, state governments are extremely unlikely to enact laws imposing religious practices in public schools. They are, on the other hand, likely to pass laws *prohibiting mandatory religious practices* in public schools. In any event, the practice of a few judges on the U.S. Supreme Court of unilaterally injecting their personal views regarding the interface between religion and government into the U.S. Constitution is oppressive.

The laws that govern that interface are a *political issue* that should be decided through the ballot box by the elected representatives of the American people, not through a constitutional amendment created by a few unelected judges. Those laws should also be subject to repeal or change by the elected representatives of the American people. If the laws passed by any federal or state legislature concerning the interface between religion and the government do not work, the people should be able to change them through a law passed by Congress, or the state legislatures. America does not have democracy in this area today because federal judges will not allow democracy.

The U.S. Supreme Court itself has stated, in declaring the actions of Congress or the President to be unconstitutional, that the strong tendency for the branches of the federal government to exceed their power *must not be permitted*. That is true even if the unconstitutional action of the President or Congress is a *good idea*. Any good idea should be made a law *only* by the government department with the power to do it, a department that is responsible to the American people through elections.

The U.S. Supreme Court put it this way in declaring an act of Congress unconstitutional and of no effect:

> "Indeed, we also have observed only recently that 'the hydraulic pressure within each of the separate Branches *to exceed the outer limits of its power*, even to accomplish *desirable objectives*, must be *resisted.*' " [15]

The foregoing principles should apply to the federal judiciary, including the U.S. Supreme Court, as much as to Congress or the President. However, there is no means to declare the actions of the U.S. Supreme Court unconstitutional, as the Supreme Court may do regarding Congress and the President.

The *only meaningful post-appointment check* against the present U.S. Supreme Court is impeachment and removal by Congress of Supreme Court judges who make constitutional law. Of course, the people can remove the members of Congress and the President from office through elections. Therefore, removal from office of judges who engage in law-making is an appropriate remedy.

The First Amendment Establishment Clause has been rewritten, and in one respect turned upside down, by a few people *without any democratic process whatsoever*. Those who engage in such despotic practices *should* be removed from office. The protection of our constitutional liberties and our democratic ideals is much more important than the career of any judge.

CHAPTER 7

THE CREATION OF THE "SEPARATION OF CHURCH AND STATE" DOCTRINE: EVERSON V. EWING BOARD OF EDUCATION

Ten year-old Melissa Sanchez came home crying. She said, "Mommy, we can't pray for Suzie at school anymore." Susan Adams was Melissa's best friend. She had leukemia.

"We'll pray more for Suzie at home. And we can still pray for her at church" said Melissa's mother, trying to comfort her.

"But I want everyone to pray for Suzie. Some of them might forget. She has been getting better since we started praying at school. Why won't our teachers let us pray anymore?" asked Melissa.

"It isn't your teachers' fault, Milly. I saw it in the newspaper. You can't pray at school anymore because the Supreme Court says so," Melissa's mother explained. "Let's pray for Suzie right now."

Melissa and her mother got on their knees and prayed

for Suzie together. Afterward, Melissa's mother started to make some cookies.

* * *

Melissa and her mother sat down to have cookies and milk. Melissa looked perplexed. Her mother asked, "What is bothering you, Milly?"

Melissa inquired, "if we can't pray for Suzie, does that mean we can't pray for President Kennedy on Fridays anymore?"

"I suppose it does," concluded her mother.

"What will keep mean people from hurting President Kennedy?" Melissa asked.

"We can still pray for him at home and at church," her mother assured her.

Among other things, the "separation of church and state" doctrine was used to exclude prayer in public schools in 1962. President John F. Kennedy was assassinated in 1963.

This chapter discusses <u>Everson v. Board of Education of Ewing Township</u> (1947) [1] which originated the "separation of church and state" doctrine. The <u>Everson</u> case's injection of the "separation of church and state" doctrine into the First Amendment violated fundamental principles of legal analysis. Also discussed in this chapter are some of the legal cases and principles that resulted from the <u>Everson</u> case, including the legal test that is used in today's Establishment Clause cases.

The Majority Opinion In *Everson*

In the <u>Everson</u> case, a local taxpayer sued to stop the reimbursement to parents, by the local school board, of the costs incurred to transport their children to and from religious schools. A New Jersey state statute permitted local school districts to pay for the transportation of school children. The local board of education applied the state statute by authorizing reimbursement of parents' expenses in sending their children to any non-profit school on public buses. Some of the parents who were reimbursed with taxpayer funds sent their children to Catholic parochial schools.

The plaintiff taxpayer claimed that the state statute, as well as the actions of the local school board, violated the First Amendment prohibition against making laws "respecting an establishment of religion." The Supreme Court majority rejected the taxpayer's position. The Supreme Court held that the First Amendment does not prohibit a general government program by which the transportation fares of school children attending *both* public and non-profit private schools (including religious schools) are reimbursed.

A slim majority of five judges held that the First Amendment:

> "[R]equires the state to be a *neutral* in its relations with groups of religious believers and non-believers . . . State power is no more to be used so as to handicap religions, than it is to favor them." [2]

I believe that the result in the Everson decision was correct under the actual language of the First Amendment, assuming, for the sake of argument, that the religion clauses apply to the states. In other words, the Everson Court correctly decided that the New Jersey statute and the reimbursement of parents' transportation costs did not violate the Establishment Clause. However, there were constitutional principles created in the Everson opinion which violated well-established legal standards and amounted to an unconstitutional amendment of the First Amendment.

The new First Amendment principles created by Everson have resulted in fundamental changes to the Establishment

Clause during the more than fifty years since <u>Everson</u> was decided. The newly-created principles in the <u>Everson</u> case were, of course, the "separation of church and state" doctrine, and the application of the Establishment Clause to state and local governments through the Fourteenth Amendment "implication" theory. As explained below, in <u>Everson</u>, the U.S. Supreme Court threw "an anchor ahead . . ." to "grapple further hold for future advances of power," as Thomas Jefferson put it. [3]

The Supreme Court stated as follows in injecting the "separation of church and state" doctrine into the First Amendment:

"In the words of *Jefferson*, the clause against establishment of religion by law was intended to erect a *'wall of separation between Church and State.'* " [4]

Later in the opinion, the Supreme Court stated as follows:

"The First Amendment has erected *a wall between church and state*. That wall *must be kept high and impregnable*. We could not approve the slightest breach. New Jersey has not breached it here." [5]

Thus, the "separation of church and state" doctrine was born.

The Dissenting Opinion In *Everson*

There were four dissenting judges in <u>Everson</u>. They also applied the new "separation of church and state" doctrine.

The dissenters took the position that the First Amendment was violated merely because people whose children were in religious schools were reimbursed for transportation expenses to and from school. The dissenters took that position even though non-religious school students' travel expenses were also reimbursed.

I have very serious problems with the views of the dissenters. They took the position that any government aid to students attending religious schools was a "law respecting an establishment of religion," even if religious and non-religious students were treated alike. That is *discrimination against religious people* who choose to include religious instruction with their children's non-religious education. These religious people should not be denied government benefits because of their religious practices. Such a law would be *hostility* by the government against religion and *an attack on the free exercise of religion*. The dissenters' view would thus have violated the Free Exercise Clause of the First Amendment, if the dissenters had prevailed. It would also have violated the "neutrality" principle articulated by the majority opinion.

Under the dissenters' principles, it would follow that the religious school children should be denied generally available police and fire protection while they attended, and traveled to and from, their religious schools. This is the logical result of the dissenters' analysis, even though the dissenters denied it. [6] It is simply unfair and unreasonable to require people to curtail their religious practices in order to receive government benefits which are available to non-religious people.

In the <u>Everson</u> case, the majority and the dissent *both* adopted the view that the First Amendment required a "separation of church and state." It is that principle which led the dissenters to their discriminatory position.

A Few Years After The *Everson* Case, The "Separation Of Church And State" Doctrine Was Used To Prohibit Long-Established State And Local Government Practices

The <u>Everson</u> case did not prohibit the state and local government actions raised in that case. However, a little more than a decade after <u>Everson</u> was decided, the U.S. Supreme Court struck down as unconstitutional religious practices in America's public schools that had been commonplace for more than one-hundred fifty years.

In <u>Engel v. Vitale</u> (1962), prayer led by officials in state-run public schools was declared unconstitutional.[7] In <u>School District of Arlington Township v. Schempp</u> (1963), Bible reading led by officials in public schools was struck down.[8] As suggested fairly recently in a 2002 U.S. Supreme Court case, prayer and Bible reading led by school officials had occurred in the state-run schools since the eighteenth century.[9]

Thus, one-hundred fifty year-old practices in state-run schools were struck down in the <u>Engel</u> case, without any change in the Constitution other than a new doctrine created by Supreme Court edict in 1947. The Supreme Court threw "an anchor ahead" to grab hold of "future advances of power" [10] in creating the "separation of church and state" doctrine.

Although I believe that *mandatory* prayer and Bible reading for religious purposes is unwise public policy, the state governments are not prohibited by the Establishment Clause from engaging in those religious practices. In my opinion, the states *should prohibit* mandatory prayer and Bible reading, in public schools, but should allow such activities on a voluntary basis. In any event, that is a political issue that is not determined by the U.S. Constitution.

The Source Of The *Everson* Court's "Separation Of Church And State" Doctrine

How did the U.S. Supreme Court come up with the "separation of church and state" concept in <u>Everson</u>? The court took the phrase out of context from a personal letter written by Thomas Jefferson to a group of religious people.

Thomas Jefferson used the phrase "wall of separation between church and state" in relation to the Establishment Clause, in order to assure the Danbury Baptists Association that the new federal government would not discriminate against them on religious grounds.[11] At that time, the Establishment Clause prohibited *only* actions by the federal government related to religion. The Fourteenth Amendment, which supposedly applied the Establishment Clause to the states, was not ratified until more than a half century later. Jefferson was making an overstatement concerning the First Amendment's scope as a politician (i.e., as President), in order to make the Danbury Baptists feel comfortable. Politicians often overstate things to please voters.

The <u>Everson</u> case extensively discussed the activities of Thomas Jefferson and James Madison as Virginia politicians to establish limited prohibitions against certain religious practices *in the State of Virginia*. They also took the phrase "wall of separation between church and state" from Thomas Jefferson's letter. Those facts are among the reasons this book quotes those two framers so extensively.

In view of the statements of Thomas Jefferson quoted earlier in this book, he would have been dismayed if he knew that the U.S. Supreme Court would, more than a century later, inject into the First Amendment a phrase he wrote in a context unrelated to determining the meaning of the First Amendment. Thomas Jefferson was vehemently opposed to such practices by the courts. For example, Jefferson was against the courts "throw[ing] an anchor ahead" to grab hold of "future advances of power," [12] as the

Supreme Court did in creating the "separation of church and state" doctrine.

Furthermore, Thomas Jefferson, James Madison, and the other founders believed that *only* the elected representatives of the American people, who had to seek reelection to stay in office, should be able to make law. That is why the Constitution has such strong separation of powers principles.

The following examples of Thomas Jefferson's behavior indicate that he did not believe the First Amendment required a "separation" between church and state, in the way the Supreme Court has applied it:

1. As U.S. President, Jefferson signed three items of federal legislation which gave land grants for the purpose of proselytizing religion among the American Indians; [13]
2. Jefferson was also the president of the District of Columbia school board, where the Bible was used as a textbook. [14]

These activities were under the control of the federal government. Therefore, if they were a "law respecting an establishment of religion" because a "separation of church and state" was required by the Establishment Clause, those actions of Thomas Jefferson were prohibited by the Establishment Clause. Obviously, Thomas Jefferson did not think so, although the "separation of church and state" doctrine would undoubtedly prohibit those actions today.

In any event, Thomas Jefferson's statement in his letter is merely that, one person's statement made several years after the First Amendment was ratified. *There were many people involved in the development of the First Amendment, and Thomas Jefferson was not one of them.* Jefferson was not a member of Congress, and was not in the United States, when the Establishment Clause was developed and approved by Congress. [15]

The <u>Everson</u> Court did not refer to any historical evidence that those involved in the development of the Establishment Clause believed that the Clause gave rise to a "separation between church and state." As explained below, the actual language of the Establishment Clause itself, as well as the record of the congressional proceedings that developed the Establishment Clause, *strongly* suggest otherwise.

The *Everson* Court's Adoption Of The "Separation Of Church And State" Doctrine Violated Fundamental Principles Of Legal Analysis

When courts try to objectively analyze legal provisions, such as constitutional provisions or statutory language, they first rely on the language of the provision itself to determine its meaning. As most courts put it, the court first looks to the "plain meaning" of the provision.

If there is any ambiguity after considering the actual language of the provision at issue, the court next considers the language of surrounding provisions. If that second level of analysis does not entirely resolve the ambiguity, the courts often look to the governmental proceedings that gave rise to the provision in question.

In the <u>Everson</u> case, the Supreme Court violated the first and primary principle by injecting the "separation of church and state" doctrine into the First Amendment. As illustrated and explained in Chapters One and Six, the "separation of church and state" principle is a broader and stronger prohibition than the actual language of the Establishment Clause (i.e., its "plain meaning"). It was, therefore, not an appropriate meaning for the Establishment Clause.

The Supreme Court in the <u>Everson</u> case then violated the second most important principle of legal analysis by ignoring the Free Exercise Clause. The Free Exercise Clause is in the same provision as the Establishment Clause and thus must be considered if the actual language does not resolve the meaning of the Establishment Clause. The <u>Everson</u> court did not consider the Free Exercise Clause in creating the "separation of church and state" doctrine. Separating church and state is such a broad prohibition, it often inhibits the free exercise of religion. Numerous recent federal court decisions illustrate this problem. A few of those decisions will be discussed in Chapters Eight and Nine.

The Supreme Court in <u>Everson</u> also did not discuss the proceedings which resulted in adopting the Establishment Clause. The record of those proceedings provides *no* support for a "separation between church and state," as explained below. In any event, the Supreme Court had already ignored the more important principles discussed above.

The Proceedings In Congress Which Derived The Establishment Clause Support Rejection Of The "Separation Of Church And State" Principle

The records of the debates and proposals in Congress which led to the Establishment Clause are not supportive of any principle in the First Amendment relating to Thomas Jefferson's phrase, "wall of separation between church and state." In fact, they *refute* such a broad construction of the Establishment Clause. The proceedings discussed and the language quoted in this section are found in the Annals of Congress, unless otherwise indicated. The Annals of Congress are a record of events in Congress.

Thomas Jefferson was not a member of Congress when the religion clauses of the First Amendment, were developed and approved by Congress. Jefferson was instead acting as a diplomat in France.[16]

James Madison was the one who spearheaded the development of the Establishment Clause in the House of Representatives. Madison proposed the following language for the Establishment Clause:

"[N]or shall any national religion be established." [17]

As the word "establishment" in the First Amendment suggests, the goal of the Establishment Clause was to prevent the establishment of a *national religion*, and to prohibit government-compelled religious observances. Madison said in the debates that the word "national" in the above-quoted phrase would "point the amendment directly to the object it was intended to prevent." [18]

Eventually, however, Madison withdrew the word "national" as a modifier of the word "religion." Madison did so in response to the concern that the word "national" may cause future Americans to believe the Constitution in general established a "national government," as opposed to a "federal government." [19] The framers did not want a national government that could exercise any governmental power it desired, but instead a federal government with limited powers. That did not change the purpose of the Establishment Clause that was articulated by Madison, however. According to the proposed language and the explanation from Madison provided above, the purpose of the Establishment Clause was to prevent the establishment of a nationwide religion by the federal government.

Two other proposals were adopted by a select committee of twelve Representatives, including Madison, and the full House of Representatives (which, of course, also included Madison), respectively, as follows:

1. "No religion shall be established by law;" [20] and
2. "Congress shall make no law establishing religion." [21]

These early proposed versions of the Establishment Clause provide further support for a narrow scope for the Establishment Clause. Congress was merely trying to prevent the federal government from sponsoring a particular religious sect and requiring adherence to specific religious practices. There was never suggestion of a "separation" between the government and religious expression.

During the debates in the House, Representative Benjamin Huntington of Connecticut was concerned that existing state-established religious denominations in the New England states may be inhibited. Huffington thus expressed his desire that the religion clauses did "not . . . patronize those who professed no religion at all." [22] As explained in this book, the Establishment Clause has been used by the U.S. Supreme Court for more than a half century to do just that.

The Senate debates regarding the Establishment Clause were secret and so were not reported in the Annals of Congress. However, the ultimate proposal of the Senate was as follows:

"Congress shall make no law establishing articles of faith or a mode of worship." [23]

Therefore, the U.S. Senate was concerned solely about forced religious beliefs or observance, not about "separating" religion and government.

After a conference between the House and the Senate, the final actual language of the Establishment Clause emerged, that is, "Congress shall make no law respecting an establishment of religion." [24] The only reasonable meaning of the Establishment Clause that could emerge from these proceedings is one prohibiting a federal religious denomination, and prohibiting federally mandated religious practices. The extremely strong and much broader prohibition that follows from "separation between church and state" has _no support_ in the Congressional proceedings.

In spite of the foregoing, what did the U.S. Supreme

Court do in the <u>Everson</u> case? The Supreme Court ignored the Annals of Congress discussed and quoted above. The Supreme Court relied almost exclusively on the experience in legislative proceedings for one of thirteen states, Virginia. In those proceedings, Virginia was enacting its *state* constitutional provisions regarding the interface between that state and religion, not any provisions for the U.S. Constitution. Not even the Virginia proceedings supported a "separation" between religion and government.

As mentioned above, at least five of the states had state government-sponsored religious denominations at that time. The <u>Everson</u> Court ignored those states' laws but extensively discussed Virginia's experience only.

Furthermore, who did the Supreme Court in the <u>Everson</u> case repeatedly rely on in its analysis of Virginia's experience? The Supreme Court relied on Thomas Jefferson, who was not in the United States when the Establishment Clause was developed and debated. The Supreme Court also relied on one other person, James Madison, whose view of the intended meaning of the federal Constitution's Establishment Clause was very narrow. As stated above, Madison thought the prohibition of a "national religion" would "point the amendment directly to the object it was intended to prevent." **25**

I do not believe the Supreme Court's many errors were accidental. The <u>Everson</u> court wanted a certain result and achieved it by violating well-established standards of legal analysis, as well as by ignoring the historical record. To state it bluntly and succinctly, the Supreme Court in the <u>Everson</u> case engaged in a form of dictatorship in creating the "separation of church and state" doctrine.

The <u>Everson</u> Court's actions were an illegal power grab by Supreme Court justices that were determined to empower themselves and future justices to impose their will on the American people. The Supreme Court succeeded because Congress failed to fulfill its duty to protect the U.S. Constitution.

The U.S. Supreme Court's "Separation Of Church And State" Doctrine Endorses Philosophical Belief Systems That Do Not Profess A Belief In A God

The U.S. Supreme Court has stated that atheism, and other forms of what will be referred to in this book as "non-believism," are belief systems which the First Amendment protects. In <u>Allegheny County v. ACLU</u> (1989), the Supreme Court said the First Amendment protects the "infidel" and the "atheist." [26] In <u>Wallace v. Jaffree</u> (1985), the Supreme Court stated that the First Amendment protects "the right to select any religious faith or none at all." [27]

As is shown below in Chapters Eight and Nine, in America today, the federal courts have in many ways endorsed "non-believism" in public institutions. Atheism and other forms of "non-believism" are belief systems based in part on negative propositions in relation to a god. In other words, "non-believism" is in part based on a belief that there is no god, or there is no reason to consider a god in relation to human affairs.

"Non-believism" is accommodated by the *absence* of any mention of a god in the public education system. As illustrated below, through the "separation of church and state" doctrine, the federal courts are exhibiting *hostility* to theistic religions (i.e., belief systems based on a belief in a god). Furthermore, the courts are also *endorsing* atheism, secular humanism and other forms of "non-believism," which are considered to be "religions" protected by the First Amendment religion clauses.

Secular Humanists And Atheists Agree That The U.S. Supreme Court Supports Their Belief Systems Through the "Separation Of Church And State" Doctrine

Lest the reader doubt the truth of the positions set forth in the preceding section, adherents to "non-believism" will be quoted here. One secular humanist writer in *The Humanist* magazine stated that his "primary hero" was the U.S. Supreme Court. In discussing the U.S. Supreme Court's impact on public education, he said:

> *"I think the most important factor moving us toward a secular society has been the educational factor.* Our schools may not teach Johnny to read properly, but the fact that Johnny is in school until he is sixteen tends to lead toward the elimination of religious superstition. . . When I was one of the editors of *The Nation* in the twenties, I wrote an editorial explaining that golf and intelligence were the two primary reasons that men did not attend church. Perhaps I would now say golf and a high school diploma." [28]

The following statements were made in the *American Atheist* publication:

> "And how does a god die? Quite simply because all his religionists have been converted to another religion, and there is no one left to make children believe they need him.
>
> Finally, it is irresistible-we must ask *how we can kill the god of Christianity. We need only insure that our schools teach only secular knowledge*; that they teach children to constantly examine and question all theories and truths put before them in any form; and that they teach nothing is proven by the number

of persons who believe a thing to be true. *If we could achieve this, god would indeed be shortly due for a funeral service.*" **29**

Thus, secular humanists and atheists believe that the decisions of our federal courts suppressing theistic religious expression, and "teach[ing] only secular knowledge" in our nation's public schools, aid their belief systems and are hostile to theistic belief systems. They are correct. That is why secularist legal organizations such as the so-called American Civil Liberties Union (known more popularly as the "ACLU") spend so much money enforcing secularism, and suppressing religious expression, through our nation's courts.

The U.S. Supreme Court professes to be "neutral" about religious issues in its First Amendment decisions. However, as shown above, *even the people who most strongly favor the Supreme Court's decisions openly admit that many federal courts are not close to being neutral.* The courts are doing the bidding of "non-believism." Many federal courts are suppressing theistic religious faiths from competing in the First Amendment's "marketplace of ideas." Examples of this kind of judicial suppression are discussed in Chapters Eight and Nine.

I do not object to discussions in the public sector (including public schools) which question, for example, Christian religious beliefs, as long as those who support those beliefs are heard. However, I have a huge problem with what the federal courts often enforce, suppression of expression about affirmative beliefs in god in public institutions. That is not "neutrality," as the adherents to "non-believism" themselves recognize. That is showing *hostility* to theistic religions and providing aid to "non-believism."

The injection of the "separation of church and state" doctrine into the First Amendment, through the <u>Everson</u>

case and its progeny, is the means for forcing "non-believism" on the American people. Some members of the federal judiciary have thus imposed their personal views, or have been induced to impose the views of non-believers, on the American people without any democratic process of any kind. They have effectively made constitutional amendments without following the democratic procedures of the constitution. That is not only unconstitutional, it is a form of dictatorship.

The "Purpose-Effect-Entanglement" Test Which Is Currently Used In Establishment Clause Cases

The cases discussed below apply what will be referred to in this book as the "purpose-effect-entanglement" test. That test is identified in most cases as the "Lemon test" because it was first created by the U.S. Supreme Court in Lemon v. Kurzman (1971).[30] The Lemon test was not created until 1971, more than twenty years after the Everson case was decided. The Supreme Court created the "purpose-effect-entanglement" test by deriving principles the Supreme Court had developed under the "separation of church and state" doctrine since the Everson case was decided in 1947.

The original Lemon test created in 1971 is similar to the test that is used by the federal courts in Establishment Clause cases today, with a modification of the second element. The current modified form is provided below.

The "purpose-effect-entanglement" test requires that a government action or statute (i.e., a law passed by the legislature) satisfy *all* of the following requirements:

1. The law or government action must have a "secular *purpose*;"
2. The law or government action must have a principal or primary *effect* that does not "endorse" or "disapprove" of religion; and

3. The law or government action must not foster an "excessive *entanglement*" with religion. [31]

The "purpose-effect-entanglement" test has been applied in the cases discussed below, either in its original form or its current modified form. Both forms of the test will be referred to as the "purpose-effect-entanglement" test.

The First Amendment's "Marketplace Of Ideas"

Religious ideas should be able to compete in the "marketplace of ideas" along with other philosophical views, whether or not the forum is a government institution. The U.S. Supreme Court agrees that the First Amendment is supposed to protect an open "marketplace" of ideas:

> "The [U.S. Supreme] Court has long viewed *the First Amendment as protecting a marketplace for the clash of different views and conflicting ideas*. That concept has been stated and restated since the Constitution was drafted." [32]

As shown by the cases discussed below, because of the illegal "separation of church and state" doctrine, the U.S. Supreme Court has violated this "marketplace of ideas" principle to which it professes to adhere. This is true even though religious ideas, unlike other kinds of concepts in the "marketplace of ideas," are *expressly* protected under the First Amendment's Free Exercise Clause. The federal courts have thus grossly distorted the First Amendment by illegally injecting the "separation of church and state" doctrine into the First Amendment.

CHAPTER 8

AN APPLICATION OF THE "SEPARATION OF CHURCH AND STATE" DOCTRINE: THE VOLUNTARY, STUDENT-LED PRAYER CASES

Jenny Collier attended Franklin High School in Littleton, Vermont. She was a bright student, a member of several clubs, and one of the finalists for the lead in the school play. Today was the day she would find out whether or not she won the part.

As she was walking to class, humming to herself, she saw Mrs. Lee, the drama teacher, beckon to her. Jenny immediately tensed up. What if she didn't get the part? What if she did?

"I need to talk to you, Jenny," said Mrs. Lee gently. "It's about the play."

Jenny was suddenly depressed. Mrs. Lee was only being nice because she had given the part to someone else. Why else would she need to see Jenny privately? She followed her teacher into an empty classroom and internally prepared herself for the news.

It was not what she was expecting.

"Your audition was wonderful, Jenny. It was funny, touching, and compelling. I would love to cast you as the lead, but...," Mrs. Lee paused. "There is a problem."

"I don't understand," said Jenny.

"It has to do with your membership in the Hope Brigade," began Mrs. Lee.

Of course, Jenny thought wearily. It has to do with the Hope Brigade. Jenny was not only a member, but one of the founders of the club. It had begun as a way to pad her extra-curricular activities for her college applications, but had gradually become more meaningful than that. The club had started out with the purpose of organizing charitable projects in the community. The members had agreed that their efforts would be most effective if they were to focus on one or two large charitable projects each school semester, rather than spreading themselves thin with many minor projects. The problem had been which charities to choose, since there were so many in need.

Jenny herself had suggested that even though they could not help every cause, they should at least keep them in their thoughts. "Kind of like sending them our hope that they will be well," she had said. And so, Hope Brigade meetings came to feature group prayers for causes like the poor, the homeless, people in war-torn countries, and even personal concerns at school, like Tommy Jones' sick father.

The school administrators, however, saw it as a risk that left them open to lawsuits. They made things very difficult for the Hope Brigade. The Brigade's meeting announce-ments were often "accidentally" left off the daily bulletin. Classrooms would often be unavailable for Hope Brigade meetings due to teacher use, other club meetings, or even cleaning.

Mrs. Lee continued, "Jenny, the school administration has informed me that I cannot cast you as the lead. The other students may feel religious pressure if they were to see that the lead actress in the school play participates in prayer meetings at school."

Frustrated, Jenny argued, "That doesn't make any sense! How's it any different from when the captain of the football team is also in the Spanish club? Is that considered pressure to learn Spanish? Or when the head cheerleader doesn't eat meat? Does that pressure students who do eat meat?"

"I'm sorry, Jenny. I can't go against school policy. I just wanted to let you know how talented I think you are, and the reason why I can't cast you in the lead role."

Defeated, Jenny thanked her teacher and left the room. It wasn't fair!

The foregoing hypothetical story was derived from a federal court opinion which stated that "[a]n adolescent may perceive 'voluntary' school prayer in a different light if he were to see . . . the leading actress in a dramatic production participating in the communal prayer meetings in the 'captive audience' setting of a school." [1] In that case, the Second Circuit Court of Appeals declared unconstitutional a student-led and student-initiated voluntary prayer group in a public school that would have met during non-school hours. That case is the first one discussed in this chapter.

About Chapters Eight and Nine

Two kinds of cases will be discussed here and in Chapter Nine. First, several cases will be addressed most of which determined that student-led, voluntary prayer or Bible study meetings in public school facilities violated the Establishment Clause. Second, several cases will be discussed, most of which found that the display in government facilities of the Ten Commandments violated the Establishment Clause.

If the reader does not wish to consider more current cases applying the "separation of church and state" doctrine, the reader should turn to Chapter Ten. Chapters Ten, Eleven and Twelve are important chapters for understanding the overall message of this book.

The Reasons For Selecting The Cases Discussed Below

I have chosen voluntary, student-led prayer cases and Ten Commandments display cases because their facts are simpler than most other Establishment Clause cases. These cases illustrate the consequences of the injection of the "separation of church and state" doctrine into the First Amendment, without requiring legal training to reasonably understand them.

An additional reason for discussing Ten Commandments display cases is that, while this book is being written, the U.S. Supreme Court has accepted two appeals in Ten Commandments display cases from two different U.S. Courts of Appeals. The decision in the resulting Supreme Court case is expected to be issued during or soon after the summer of 2005.

It should be understood that, except for extremely rare situations not relevant here, an appeal from a Court of Appeals decision has to be voluntarily selected by the U.S. Supreme Court. There is generally no right to appeal to the U.S. Supreme Court. However, the losing party has a right to appeal from the U.S. District Courts to the U.S. Courts of Appeals.

Most of the cases discussed below are from the U.S. Courts of Appeals because it is rare for the U.S. Supreme Court to decide an Establishment Clause case. Moreover, comparing the facts and principles of Supreme Court cases with divergent fact patterns would be confusing, especially for a non-lawyer. Easier comparisons can be made for cases with similar facts.

The Court of Appeals cases discussed below regarding voluntary, student-led prayer cases were later effectively overruled by a Supreme Court case, which is also discussed below. Nevertheless, these Court of Appeals cases illustrate the disregard of the actual language of the Establishment Clause, and the Free Exercise Clause, that often results from the "separation of church and state" doctrine.

Brandon v. Guilderland Board of Education

In Brandon v. Board of Education of Guilderland Central School District (1980), religious public school students were denied by public school officials the right to voluntarily meet in classrooms for prayer during non-school hours. The students sued the school district alleging, among other things, a violation of the Free Exercise clause, and their right under the First Amendment to freedom of speech.

The Brandon Court held that the students' right to *freely exercise their religious beliefs* was *not* violated. The Brandon Court also held that even if their Free Exercise Clause rights had been violated, *the Establishment Clause would override their freedom of religious expression.* Finally, the Brandon Court held that the students' right to *free speech* was *not* violated. [1]

The Alleged Violation Of The Students' Free Exercise Of Religion In *Brandon*

The Second Circuit Court's first conclusion was that "the *free exercise rights* of the Students for Voluntary Prayer were *not limited* by the Guilderland School District's *refusal to permit* communal prayer meetings to occur on school premises." [2] That statement is internally contradictory because a "refusal to permit" activity is a *limitation* on that activity, namely the students' prayer. The Brandon Court did not give any plausible reason why the denial of the students' right to pray at the school was not a limitation on their right to freely exercise their religion.

The Second Circuit Court said that the religious students

could worship at a different location, such as at a church, in an attempt to justify its conclusion that there was no limitation on the students' free exercise of their religious beliefs. [3] This position showed *a bias against religious freedom and religious speech* because it was a "time and place restriction" on religious speech. A "time and place restriction," such as not allowing the students to pray at the public school outside of classroom hours, is rarely tolerated by the federal courts in other areas of speech, such as political speech.

For example, public university student protestors can, as a practical matter, always conduct their political protest rallies away from the university campus. However, a restriction on student protestors speech *at the university* is protected by the First Amendment's freedom of speech clause, unless there is a compelling state interest to overcome the right to free speech. [4] The <u>Brandon</u> Court's bias against religious speech was particularly egregious because religious speech is *expressly* protected by the First Amendment Free Exercise Clause, unlike other forms of speech (such as political speech).

The Court then concluded that the students' right to freely exercise their religion was not violated because "*the students have made no showing* that they lack other facilities for communal prayer." [5] A major problem with this analysis is it put the *burden* of justifying the free exercise of religion at the public school *on the students*. The <u>Brandon</u> Court had previously admitted that *the burden is on the government* to show a "compelling interest" supporting the restriction on "free exercise" of religion. The <u>Brandon</u> Court's bias against religious speech was thus compounded by the Second Circuit Court's application of the wrong legal standard.

The "Compelling Interest" That Supposedly Justified The *Brandon* Court's Suppression Of Voluntary Student-Led Prayer Was The "Separation of Church And State" Doctrine

The Brandon Court then proceeded to find that, assuming for the sake of argument that the free exercise of religion was violated, there was a "compelling state interest" to justify the limitation. According to the Court, the "compelling state interest" was the Establishment Clause, which would have been violated if the voluntary student prayer had been permitted.

The Second Circuit Court concluded that allowing voluntary, student-led prayer in a public school is a "law respecting an establishment of religion," because such prayer created an "unconstitutional link between church and state." The Court then implemented the "separation of church and state" doctrine by applying the "purpose-effect-entanglement" test. [6]

The Second Circuit Court weighted the judge-made "separation of church and state" doctrine, which is *not* in the First Amendment, more heavily than the "free exercise" of religion, which *is* in the First Amendment.

The *Brandon* Court's Violations Of Its Version Of Commonly-Held American Principles

The Brandon Court did not even follow its own principles. To begin its analysis, the Second Circuit Court stated as follows:

> "To many Americans, the state's noblest function is the education of our nation's youth. We entrust this responsibility largely to the public schools, and hope our children grow into responsible citizens by learning the enduring values of Western Civilization we all share – an appreciation of *critical reasoning*, a

commitment to *democratic institutions*, and a dedication to principles of *fairness*." [7]

Unfortunately, what followed in the <u>Brandon</u> Court's opinion violated all of the principles expressed by the Court. "Critical reasoning" was lacking in several ways. As explained above, the Court contradicted itself, used reasoning that went against well-established First Amendment principles, was blinded by bias against religious expression, and applied a wrong legal standard.

Instead of adhering to "democratic institutions," the opinion relied upon illegal judge-made constitutional law (i.e., the "separation of church and state" doctrine), which was created without any democratic process whatsoever.

Finally, there was nothing "fair" about excluding students from engaging in voluntary, student-led prayer during non-school hours. Those students' parents paid taxes to pay for the public schools along with other non-religious parents of other public school students. Separately, it was completely unfair to exclude those students' speech based on its religious content. Restrictions on speech based on its content give rise to heightened protection for other kinds of speech, in First Amendment cases.

The *Brandon* Court's Bias Against Theistic Religion

The Second Circuit Court also stated as follows in <u>Brandon</u>:

"Our nation's elementary and secondary schools play a unique role in transmitting basic and fundamental values to our youth. To an impressionable student, even *the mere appearance of secular involvement in religious activities might indicate that the state has placed its imprimatur on a particular religious creed. This symbolic inference is too dangerous to permit. . . .* An adolescent may perceive 'voluntary' school prayer in a different light if he were to see the captain of the school's football team, the student president, or the leading actress in a dramatic production participating in the communal prayer meetings in the 'captive audience' setting of a school." [8]

The Court's comments about what "might" be the perceptions of public school students were pure speculation. *No evidence* was cited to support the Court's position. If anything, common sense suggests that high school students do not perceive the discussions in voluntary student clubs to be endorsed by the public school when they are not initiated by school officials. In excluding voluntary student-led prayer, the <u>Brandon</u> Court showed its bias against theistic religion, and its favoritism to "non-believism."

The "Separation Of Church And State" Doctrine Gives Judges The Power To Be Oppressive To Religious People

The <u>Brandon</u> Court acknowledged that the "inflexible" separation of church and state would threaten the free exercise of religion. In fact, as discussed above, the <u>Brandon</u> Court said that, if the "strict" or "inflexible" construction of the "separation of church and state" doctrine is applied, *religious schools and churches would be denied police and fire protection.* [9]

How is the degree of "flexibility" in the "separation of church and state" doctrine determined in a particular case? It is determined by the personal views of federal judges. Thomas Jefferson would have shuddered at such a thought, but that is what has happened.

Fortunately, the Second Circuit Court's ultimate decision in <u>Brandon</u> was effectively overruled by the U.S.

Supreme Court in 1990. The 1990 decision is discussed at the end of this chapter. However, <u>Brandon</u> reveals where the unconstitutional "separation of church and state" doctrine leads, to the blatant denial of both the free exercise of religion and the freedom of speech found in the First Amendment.

Lubbock CLU v. Lubbock School District

In <u>Lubbock Civil Liberties Union v. Lubbock Independent School District</u>, (1982),[10] the Fifth Circuit Court of Appeals declared unconstitutional, under the Establishment Clause, the following policy of a local public school board:

> "4. The School Board *permits students to gather* at the school with supervision either before or after regular school hours *on the same basis as other groups* as determined by the school administration to meet *for any educational, moral, religious or ethical purposes* so long as attendance at such meetings is *voluntary*." [11]

The Fifth Circuit Court concluded that this school board policy violated the Establishment Clause.

The Fifth Circuit Court applied the "purpose-effect-entanglement" test in striking down the policy. The Court concluded that all three elements of the "purpose-effect-entanglement" test were violated, although the violation of only one element was necessary.

The Application Of The "Secular Purpose" Test In The *Lubbock* Case

According to the Fifth Circuit Court, the public school's Paragraph 4 policy did not have the required "secular purpose" (i.e., the first element of the "purpose-effect-entanglement" test) because:

> "*[T]he purpose of this policy*, ostensibly devised to allow many groups to meet, is, when examined in the context to the total school policy, more clearly *designed to allow the meetings of religious groups*. The District's justification for the religious meetings, the development of leadership and communicative skills, *cannot withstand scrutiny when these goals can be attained through non-religious student associations*." [12]

I concur with the Court that the Paragraph 4 policy was designed to allow religious groups at the public schools in question to meet. However, they were to meet on a voluntary, student-led basis. Because the religious groups were only allowed to meet on the same non-religious basis as non-religious groups, the reason for that policy was clearly secular, not religious.

Furthermore, the policy was created because the ACLU of Lubbock, Texas had previously brought a lawsuit against the school board concerning an earlier policy. Therefore, the school board issued the policy for the additional "secular purpose" of meeting Establishment Clause standards. The Lubbock Court drew the opposite conclusion.

The Application Of The "Effects" Test In *Lubbock*

The Fifth Circuit Court then went on to apply the "effects" element of the "purpose-effect-entanglement" test. In concluding that the school board's policy in Paragraph 4 had the "primary effect" of favoring religion, the Court stated as follows:

> "[T]he critical factors are the District's use of its *compulsory education machinery*, which provides

students available to attend even voluntary meetings, and its *implicit support and approval of the religious meetings.*" [13]

The school district's compulsory education laws were completely irrelevant to the policy. The policy made the religious meetings voluntary and student-run. Students were not being compelled to do anything religious. Compulsory attendance at the public school was solely a result of secular requirements to attend school.

Nor was there any "implicit support and approval of the religious meetings." The religious meetings were conducted on a voluntary basis that was equally available to other secular kinds of meetings. The Fifth Circuit Court was attacking speech based upon its religious content, which is usually strongly prohibited by the First Amendment.

The Application Of The "Entanglement" Element In *Lubbock*

The Fifth Circuit Court then went on to find that there was an "excessive entanglement" with religion in the school board's policy. The reasoning for the Fifth Circuit Court's decision here was that *supervision* of the public school students was required by the policy. However, the need for supervision arose only because the students were required to attend school for secular reasons.

The *Lubbock* Decision Was Not Supported By The First Amendment

The Lubbock decision illustrates again the inappropriateness of the "separation of church and state" doctrine. Voluntary, student-led prayer meetings are clearly not a "law respecting an establishment of religion." They involve religious *expression*, but not an *establishment* of religion.

Prohibition of voluntary religious expression was an

impermissible "time and place restriction" on religious speech. Therefore, the Fifth Circuit Court itself violated the First Amendment in its decision.

Bender v. Willamsport Area School District

In <u>Bender v. Williamsport Area School District</u> (1984),[14] students attending a high school in Williamsport, Pennsylvania sued the local school district for not allowing them to continue meeting on a voluntary basis to conduct student-led Bible reading and prayer in school facilities. The student meetings had been, and were to be, held during a 30-minute activity period on Tuesdays and Thursdays during which other student groups also met.

The *Bender* Court's Overall Analysis

The Third Circuit Court of Appeals first concluded that the students' constitutional *free speech rights* expressly given in the First Amendment *were violated*. The free speech violation was, therefore, permitted only if the school district could show a "compelling state interest" in prohibiting the students' speech.

Second, the Court decided that *the Establishment Clause would have been violated* if the school district had allowed the students to conduct voluntary, student-led prayer and Bible reading. The Court applied the "purpose-effect-entanglement" test in determining the potential Establishment Clause violation.

Finally, the Third Circuit Court decided that the potential Establishment Clause violation was a "compelling state interest" which *justified the violation* of the students' right to free speech.

The *Bender* Court's Improper Justifications For Allowing The Students' "Free Speech" Rights To Be Violated

The <u>Bender</u> Court gave the following reasons for its conclusion that the potential violation of the Establishment Clause justified a violation of the students' right to free speech:

1. A public high school is a "limited forum" for exercising free speech rights (i.e., student activities are subject to the permission of public school officials);
2. The students had places other than public school to pray and conduct in Bible reading;
3. "Public schools have never been a forum for religious expression;" and
4. Allowing the students to exercise their free speech rights would "promote an impermissible atmosphere of religious partisanship" resulting in "divisiveness." [15]

Regarding reason number one identified above, the most glaring error in the Third Circuit Court's analysis is that it completely ignored the Free Exercise Clause. In deciding whether the Establishment Clause was a "compelling state interest," the Court should have weighed the students' right to free exercise of religion against the Establishment Clause. What was at issue was voluntary, student-led prayer and Bible study, an activity that fits squarely within the language of the Free Exercise Clause. In addition, the <u>Bender</u> Court was weighting the "separation of church and state" doctrine, which is not in the First Amendment, more heavily than free speech, which is in the First Amendment.

The second reason for the Third Circuit Court's decision that is listed above was also inappropriate. As discussed in connection with the <u>Brandon</u> case, the availability of other places for the students to pray or read the Bible does not justify the violation of two other clauses of the First Amendment, the Free Exercise and Free Speech Clauses. "Time and place restrictions" are disfavored under the First Amendment. The students should not be prohibited from voluntarily exercising their rights to the free exercise of religion and to free speech during their school's activity period, while they were compelled to attend the public school.

The Third Circuit Court was factually in error in saying that the public schools have never been a place for religious expression (the third reason listed above). As three justices of the U.S. Supreme Court have more recently suggested, prayer and Bible study were *required* in the nations' public schools from the time the First Amendment was ratified until the 1960's. [16]

Furthermore, with respect to "divisiveness" (the fourth reason listed above), there is *nothing* divisive about voluntary, student-led prayer and Bible study. What is divisive is the Third Circuit Court's favoritism toward secular humanism, and other forms of "non-believism," in prohibiting voluntary theistic religious expression. Religious students in public school were muzzled here by the so-called protectors of individual rights, federal judges.

The *Bender* Court's Analysis Reveals The Futility Of "Separation Of Church And State" Principles

There was another aspect of the Third Circuit Court's analysis in Bender that exposed the inconsistency and unfairness of the principles currently applied in Establishment Clause cases. In the <u>Bender</u> case, the religious students argued that their meetings were *non-denominational* and, therefore, not "divisive." In rejecting the students' argument, the Court stated as follows:

"Indeed, if *the courts* were to establish the degree of sectarianism as a part of the Establishment Clause tests, then *they would themselves be engaging in impermissible entanglement by the very act of applying those tests*, since it is not appropriate in this context for the judiciary to evaluate contrasting theologies . . . . Making a . . . determination as to whether such activity is *partial to a particular sect* is *well beyond the pale of judicial functions.*" [17]

Thus, the Third Circuit Court admitted that it would violate the Establishment Clause by "entangling" itself with religion, if it decided "whether such activity [i.e., the students' voluntary non-denominational meetings] is *partial* to a particular sect [i.e., a particular religious belief system]." But the federal courts often decide whether religious activity is "partial to" one sect or the other, in striking down "religious" expression in public institutions.

Specifically, the federal courts often determine whether a state government law or practice would be "partial to" a theistic sect, such as Christianity or Judaism, and would be partial *against* non-theistic sects, such as atheism and secular humanism. The Bender court did so in using "religious partisanship" and "divisiveness" as a basis for its decision against the student adherents to a theistic religion. [See reason number four above.] The U.S. Supreme Court has determined that non-theistic sects such as atheism are "religions" protected by the religion clauses of the First Amendment. [18] Therefore, *by its own admission*, the Bender Court's decision itself violated the Establishment Clause in applying the "purpose-effect-entanglement" test by "engaging in an impermissible entanglement" with non-theistic "religions." The Bender Court's analysis was admittedly "well beyond the pale of judicial functions."

The Bender case was later disapproved in two other

Third Circuit Court of Appeals decisions in 1993 and 2003, due to the 1990 Supreme Court decision discussed below. [19]

To summarize, the problems in the Brandon, Lubbock and Bender cases that are discussed above illustrate the unfairness of both the "separation of church and state" doctrine and the current legal test that was derived from that doctrine, the "purpose-effect-entanglement" test. Furthermore, even though those cases came to the same final result, their analyses were not consistent. For example, Brandon and Bender disagreed whether it would be a violation of the Free Speech Clause to stop voluntary, student-led prayer or Bible study. Brandon found there was no violation of free speech, but Bender disagreed. Those cases, however, agreed that any such violation was justified due to the "separation of church and state" doctrine.

The Equal Access Act and *Westside Board of Education v. Mergens*

After the Brandon, Lubbock and Bender cases were decided, Congress enacted a set of laws in 1984 called the Equal Access Act ("EAA"). The EAA sought to require public schools across the nation to allow access to religious student groups on the same basis as non-religious groups.

It should be understood that, because the decisions in the Brandon, Lubbock and Bender cases were based on the First Amendment, the EAA did not initially affect the decisions in those cases. As explained in Chapter Five, constitutional law, such as that found in the First Amendment, is superior to any law passed by Congress.

In Board of Education of the Westside Community Schools v. Mergens (1990), [20] public school students sued the school board which was overseeing a public high school in Omaha, Nebraska. The students sued because the school board would not allow them to have a Bible study group under the EAA. The Bible study group would have met on the same basis as other non-religious student groups.

The U.S. Supreme Court held that the EAA applied to the students' request for permission to meet as a Bible study group. The Supreme Court also held that the EAA and the students' request did *not* violate the Establishment Clause. Therefore, the school district should have allowed the students to have their proposed religious meetings. The Mergens case effectively overruled the decisions in the Brandon, Lubbock, and Bender cases discussed above.

Only the Supreme Court's consideration of the Establishment Clause will be discussed here. In deciding that the Establishment Clause was not violated by the EAA, or its proposed application at Westside High School, the Supreme Court filed *three separate opinions* of different justices.

The Application Of The "Purpose-Effect-Entanglement" Test In *Mergens* By A Plurality Of Four Justices

The plurality opinion of *four* Supreme Court justices applied the "purpose-effect-entanglement" test. The plurality first decided that the EAA, and the proposed application of the EAA at the public school by the religious students, had a "secular purpose." The secular purpose was declared by Congress as follows: To avoid discrimination against religious and other types of speech. In finding a secular purpose, the Supreme Court stated that failing to provide equal access to religious students would "demonstrate not neutrality, but hostility toward religion." [21]

The four-judge plurality opinion next considered whether the "effect" of the EAA, and its proposed application by the religious students, was to "endorse" religion. The plurality concluded there was no endorsement effect for the following reasons:

1. High school students would not perceive an endorsement of religion because the religious student groups were permitted to engage in *private* (not governmental) speech on a basis that *did not discriminate against other non-religious groups*;
2. The EAA prohibited participation of public school officials in the religious student meetings and the meetings were *voluntary*; and
3. Other *non-religious groups* were permitted to, and actually did, meet at the school on the *same basis.* [22]

Finally, the plurality concluded there was no "excessive entanglement" with religion because school officials were not allowed to, and would not, participate in or direct the meetings of the religious groups. School officials' maintenance of order at the meetings did not entangle the school with religious activities. Furthermore, people from outside the school were not permitted to participate in the meetings. [23]

The only problems I have with the plurality opinion was its use of the unconstitutional "purpose-effect-entanglement" test, and its reliance on the absence of non-school persons from the students' voluntary religious meetings, as a partial basis for finding no Establishment Clause violation. Allowing outside religious leaders, for example, to participate in purely *voluntary* student meetings is not a law or practice by the government regarding an *establishment* of religion. The parents of these religious students pay taxes to pay for the public school facilities on the same basis as the parents of non-religious students. It is the unconstitutional "separation of church and state" doctrine that results in exclusion of religious leaders from participating in voluntary meetings on public school campuses. [24] Of course, atheist students and other adherents to "non-believievsm" should also be permitted to have non-school speakers on a voluntary basis.

The First Concurring Opinion Of Two Justices In *Mergens*

In the first concurring opinion of two judges, there was no Establishment Clause violation because:

1. The EAA did not " 'give direct benefits to religion' " so as to establish a state religion or religious faith, or tend to do so; and
2. The school did not "coerce any student to participate in a religious activity." [25]

These reasons track the meaning of the actual language of the Establishment Clause (assuming, for the sake of argument, that the federal courts have the power to prohibit *state* government actions under the First Amendment). This reasoning also balances the Establishment Clause with the Free Exercise Clause by avoiding any hostility to religion.

The Second Concurring Opinion Of Two Justices In *Mergens*

The second concurring opinion of two different judges stated that, under the Free Speech Clause, the school was prohibited from excluding the students' speech based on its *religious content*, when other students' speech was permitted.

The second concurring opinion also held that the school had to take *affirmative measures* to ensure no perception of the high school students that the school endorsed the religious groups. The school could do this by not encouraging the students' clubs to meet, and making it clear that the student clubs were not related to the school's mission. Alternatively, the school could specifically deny any endorsement of the religious clubs in particular. [26]

This analysis is an outgrowth of the "separation of church and state" doctrine, not the Establishment Clause. These judges, as have the federal courts in general, focused on their speculations about perceptions among public school students of the school's implied approval of religion. Such implied approval, even if it existed, is not a law regarding an *establishment* of religion.

In addition, the second concurring opinion ignored the Free Exercise Clause. The religious students were obviously seeking to exercise their freedom of religious expression, which is supposed to be guaranteed by the First Amendment.

Conclusion

To conclude, voluntary student-led prayer and Bible study in public schools should *never* have been seriously considered as a potential violation of the Establishment Clause. Permitting such activity clearly does not involve an "establishment" of religion. But several courts held otherwise due to the consequences of the judge-made "separation of church and state" doctrine, and in some instances, the strong bias against theistic religion of some federal judges. It is a travesty of American constitutional law and justice that three federal Court of Appeals cases found voluntary, student-led prayer or Bible study in public schools to be a violation of the Establishment Clause.

It is fortunate that these cases were effectively overruled by the <u>Mergens</u> case. However, the unconstitutional "separation of church and state" doctrine and its derivation, the "purpose-effect-entanglement" test, remain as current constitutional law, according to the U.S. Supreme Court. Those judge-made constitutional principles should be eliminated from our nation's law.

CHAPTER 9

ANOTHER APPLICATION OF THE "SEPARATION OF CHURCH AND STATE" DOCTRINE: THE TEN COMMANDMENTS DISPLAY CASES

━┼══┼━

This chapter discusses cases involving Ten Commandments displays in government facilities, including two Court of Appeals cases related to the highly publicized controversy concerning Alabama Supreme Court Justice Roy Moore. The Ten Commandments display in that situation was found to be unconstitutional.

The only U.S. Supreme Court case on the issue to date is the earliest case. The display was found by the Supreme Court to be unconstitutional.

Two Court of Appeals cases, which are presently on appeal before by the U.S. Supreme Court, are also discussed. In one case, the display was declared unconstitutional. The other case upheld the display as constitutional. The Supreme Court is scheduled to make its decision during July 2005.

There have been eight other Court of Appeals cases regarding Ten Commandments displays. Five of those additional cases declared the Ten Commandments displays to be unconstitutional. Three other cases found the displays to be permissible under the First Amendment. The most important distinction appears to be the length of time the displays have been in place.

These cases illustrate the futility of the "separation of church and state" doctrine, and the biased decision-making against faiths that profess a belief in a god resulting from the "separation of church and state" doctrine.

Stone v. Graham: The First Case To Prohibit A Ten Commandments Display

In <u>Stone v. Graham</u> (1980), the U.S. Supreme Court struck down as unconstitutional a Kentucky statute requiring the posting of the Ten Commandments on the walls of public school classrooms. [1]

The Supreme Court's Overall Analysis In *Stone*

In <u>Stone</u>, the Supreme Court held that the Kentucky law related to an "establishment of religion" and was therefore prohibited by the First Amendment. The U.S. Supreme Court applied the "purpose-effect-entanglement" test it had previously created in the <u>Lemon</u> case, in striking down the Kentucky law. That test is discussed in Chapter 7.

The Supreme Court concluded that the Ten Commandments posting statute had a non-secular purpose (element (1) of the "purpose-effect-entanglement" test), and was thus unconstitutional. This was true even though *the state legislature expressly declared a secular purpose for the statute* when it was enacted. Furthermore, the following statement was required by the statute to be posted on the wall: "The secular application of the Ten Commandments is clearly seen in its adoption as the fundamental legal code of Western Civilization and the Common Law of the United States." [2]

The U.S. Supreme Court was unable to point to any

evidence of the non-secular purpose of the posting, other than the contents of the Ten Commandments themselves, which "do not confine themselves to arguably secular matters." [3] According to the Court, in addition to secular matters, the Ten Commandments refer to "religious duties of believers: worshipping the Lord God alone, not using the Lord's name in vain, and observing the Sabbath Day." [4]

Of course, the Ten Commandments will always have these elements if they are provided in their entirety. Therefore, if <u>Stone</u>, is followed, a display of the Ten Commandments in their entirety may never have a "secular purpose."

The Relationship Of The Historical And Educational Significance Of The Ten Commandments To The *Stone* Case

It is ironic that, when the U.S. Supreme Court held the oral argument for the <u>Stone</u> decision, a depiction of Moses holding the Ten Commandments was (and still is) posted above its members in the U.S. Supreme Court building. [5]

The <u>Stone</u> Court did not discuss the obvious historical importance of the Ten Commandments to the law of Western Civilization, and the "common law" of at least some states of America. The "common law" is referred to in the Seventh Amendment of the Bill of Rights. The "common law" of America is derived from similar laws first developed in the courts of England. The Bible is called by some American authorities the foundation of the "common law." [6] Since the Ten Commandments are the most foundational legal code of the Bible, their historical significance regarding the "common law" provided a secular purpose for the display, in spite of the Supreme Court's contrary decision.

The historical importance of the Ten Commandments to the law of this country and Western Civilization is inescapable. The U.S. Supreme Court should not be permitted to prohibit the facts of history from being posted on the walls of governmental facilities through the application of the judicially-created "separation of church and state" doctrine. That is true even if those facts have religious elements. Such a prohibition may be appropriate in an Orwellian-type society in which a "Big Brother" government suppresses and systematically changes history. However, it is not appropriate in a democracy, such as the United States of America. The people of America should be able to vote to elect or remove the government officials who decide these issues, not be controlled by the judicial edicts of nine or fewer unelected Supreme Court judges.

In the <u>Stone</u> decision, the U.S. Supreme Court claimed that posting the Ten Commandments on the walls of public school classrooms "serves no . . . educational function." [7] However, historical documents are frequently displayed on public school classrooms and other government facilities, whether or not they have religious references. One of those documents is the Declaration of Independence, written by Thomas Jefferson, which refers to the "Creator," "Nature's God," "the Supreme Judge of the World" and "Divine Providence."

In view of these religious references, the Declaration of Independence does not "confine [itself] . . . to arguably secular matters," as the <u>Stone</u> Court put it in discussing the Ten Commandments. However, the Declaration of Independence clearly has secular significance in American history. Ten Commandments displays are also clearly educational, although apparently not the kind of educational material that these Supreme Court judges desired America's children to see.

Would the U.S. Supreme Court claim that religious historical writings or artifacts that are displayed on the walls of a museum are not educational? For example, would the

U.S. Supreme Court strike down as unconstitutional the display of American Indian religious artifacts and sayings on the walls of national park museums? Of course, the answer to both questions today is no. The reason the U.S. Supreme Court denied the educational value of posting the Ten Commandments was its bias in favor of "non-believism" and against Christianity and Judaism. These judges' personal views should not be injected into our country's constitutional law, but they are at this time in our nation's history.

The *Stone* Case Shows How The 'Purpose-Effect-Entanglement" Test Is Biased In Favor Of Non-Theistic Belief Systems

The <u>Stone</u> case illustrates how the "purpose-effect-entanglement" test violates the principle of "neutrality" toward religion first set forth in <u>Everson</u>. The U.S. Supreme Court has declared what has been coined "non-believism" in its various forms, to be protected "religious" systems under the Establishment Clause of the First Amendment.

By way of reminder, in <u>Wallace v. Jaffree</u> (1985), the U.S. Supreme Court said: "[T]he Court has unambiguously concluded that the individual freedom of conscience protected by the First Amendment embraces *the right to select any religious faith or none at all.*" [8] Similarly, in <u>Allegheny County v. ACLU</u> (1989), the U.S. Supreme Court said that the Establishment Clause is "recognized as guaranteeing religious liberty and equality to the *infidel*, the *atheist*, or the adherent of a non-Christian faith such as Islam or Judaism." [9]

Therefore, since the Establishment Clause protects "any religious faith or none at all," it protects all forms of what I have coined as "non-believism," including atheism and secular humanism. Secular humanism is defined in the dictionary as a "philosophy or world view that stresses human values without reference to religion or spirituality." [10]

As illustrated by the <u>Stone</u> case, the first part of the "purpose-effect-entanglement" test requires that a government action "have a secular . . . purpose." This first element of the judicially-created test for the Establishment Clause is biased heavily in favor of *secular* humanism and other forms of "non-believism." Therefore, the test violates the principle of "neutrality" toward "religion" first articulated in the *Everson* case.

Suppose the first part of the "purpose-effect-entanglement" test was that the government action "must have a *godly* purpose" to be constitutional, instead of a *secular* purpose. Secular humanists, atheists and other "non-believism" adherents would vehemently oppose such a standard. They would claim that the Supreme Court illegally changed the First Amendment, and was biasing the Constitution in favor of Christianity, Judaism and other theistic religions. They would be correct. For the same reason, this book is correct in claiming that the Supreme Court's "secular purpose" test is biased in favor of "non-believism."

Glassroth v. Moore and McGinely v. Houston: The Alabama Ten Commandments Monument Cases

The following discussion relates to the highly publicized dispute concerning the placement of a Ten Commandments monument in front of the Alabama State Judicial Building during 2003. The monument was placed by Roy S. Moore, the former Chief Justice of the Alabama Supreme Court. Justice Moore was involuntarily removed from office because he refused to remove the Ten Commandments monument after being ordered to do so by a federal judge.

The two cases that will be discussed here are named <u>Glassroth v. Moore</u> (2003) and <u>McGinely v. Houston</u> (2004). [11] These cases are discussed here because they illustrate some of the reasons for the futility of the "separation of church and state" doctrine, and the "purpose-effect-entan-glement" test, which is used to analyze Establishment Clause cases. The U.S. Supreme Court will not consider the Glassroth and McGinely cases on appeal.

The *Glassroth* Case

In Glassroth, the placement of the Ten Commandments monument by Chief Justice Moore was determined to be a violation of the Establishment Clause. One of Justice Moore's arguments against the lower court's decision in Glassroth depended on his proposed definition of "religion" for the purpose of applying the Establishment Clause. The Eleventh Circuit Court rejected Justice Moore's definition of "religion" and stated:

> "The Supreme Court has instructed us that for First Amendment purposes *religion includes* non-Christian faiths and those that do not profess belief in the Judeo-Christian God; indeed, it includes *lack of any faith* . . . . *Chief Justice Moore's proffered definition of religion is inconsistent with the Supreme Court's because he presupposes a belief in God.* We understand that the Chief Justice disagrees with *the Supreme Court's definition of religion*, but we are bound by it." [12]

Thus, "the Supreme Court's definition of religion" under the Establishment Clause includes "the lack of any faith" in a god, according to the Eleventh Circuit Court in Glassroth. These statements by the Eleventh Circuit Court are inconsistent with the McGinely decision by the same Eleventh Circuit Court, which is discussed below.

The *McGinely* Case

In McGinely, the plaintiff claimed that *the removal of*

Justice Moore's Ten Commandments monument pursuant to the decision in the <u>Glassroth</u> case, was *a violation of the Establishment Clause.* The plaintiff argued that the removal of the monument was a violation of the Establishment Clause because it was an *endorsement of non-theistic religion or faith* (i.e., a belief system having no reference to any god). The Eleventh Circuit Court rejected that argument in stating that the U.S. Supreme Court has *not* determined whether " 'secular humanism is a religion for purposes of the Establishment Clause.' " [13]

If the dictionary definition of "secular humanism" was intended in the Court's position quoted above, the Eleventh Circuit Court *did not respond* to the plaintiff's argument. The plaintiff's argument in the <u>McGinely</u> case referred to "non-theistic" belief systems *in general, not only "secular humanism."* According to the dictionary definition of "secular humanism" provided above, "secular humanism" is only one type of "non-believism." For example, atheism (i.e., the belief that there is *no* god) is different from "secular humanism" (i.e., human values *without reference* to a god). Therefore, the plaintiff's argument was that non-theistic belief systems such as atheism (in addition to secular humanism) were favored by removal of the Ten Commandments display. As explained above, the Supreme Court has specifically determined atheism to be a protected "religion" under the Establishment Clause. The Eleventh Circuit Court thus did not address the favoritism to, for example, atheism that resulted from removal of the Ten Commandments display.

It is possible the Eleventh Circuit Court's understanding of "secular humanism" included *all* non-theistic belief systems. If so, its statement that the Supreme Court has not yet decided whether "religion" under the Establishment Clause includes "secular humanism" would be is inconsistent with the same Court's position in the <u>Glassroth</u> case.

The Eleventh Circuit Court's position would also be wrong. As explained above, the same Eleventh Circuit Court correctly stated in <u>Glassroth</u> that the term "religion" in the Establishment Clause includes "the lack of any faith" in a god, citing U.S. Supreme Court cases. [14] Therefore, according to the Eleventh Circuit Court itself, the U.S. Supreme Court has decided that "secular humanism" in this broader sense is a "religion" under the Establishment Clause.

I believe the Eleventh Circuit Court effectively failed to address the question raised by the plaintiff in <u>McGinely</u> because it had no reasonable response. The federal Courts of Appeals are put in very difficult positions when they have to apply the Supreme Court's "separation of church and state" principle, along with other inconsistent judge-made principles supposedly derived from the Establishment Clause.

McGinely Reveals The Futility of The Supreme Court's Establishment Clause Standards

The <u>McGinely</u> Court also made some statements that show the *futility* of the "separation of church and state" doctrine in general, and the "purpose-effect-entanglement" test in particular. The statements were as follows:

> "In this case the appellants contend that the removal of the Ten Commandments monument created empty space, and that this empty space violates the Establishment Clause because it is an *endorsement* of religion, or in this instance, non-theism. This argument is without merit. If the appellants were correct in their assertion an Establishment Clause violation could never be cured because *every time a violation is found and cured by the removal of the statute or practice that cure itself would violate the Establishment Clause* by leaving behind empty space." [15]

In this paragraph, the Eleventh Circuit Court identified a problem that is raised by the plaintiff's position in the case. However, the problem identified, namely that an Establishment Clause violation occurred no matter what the Court did, is caused by the futile legal standards created by the U.S. Supreme Court, not by the plaintiff's argument. The "separation of church and state" doctrine is unworkable because of the Supreme Court's broad definition of "religion" under the First Amendment, and its mandate for the government to maintain a "neutral" position regarding "religious" views.

To summarize, since the definition of "religion" under the Establishment Clause includes faith in a god, as well as the *absence* of faith in a god, no matter what the Supreme Court does in an Establishment Clause case, it will usually favor one "religion" or another. "Neutrality" is usually impossible.

The "Purpose-Effect-Entanglement Test Has Been Criticized By Most Of The Current Members Of The U.S. Supreme Court

This book is not the first place that the "purpose-effect entanglement" test has been criticized. In fact, at least six of the nine current member of the U.S. Supreme Court have criticized the test. [16]

The closest criticism to the ones made here is that of Chief Justice Rehnquist. He stated that "the <u>Lemon</u> test [i.e., the "purpose-effect-entanglement" test] has no more grounding in the history of the First Amendment than does the wall theory [i.e., the "separation of church and state" theory] upon which it rests." [17]

The Wisdom of Some "Separation of Church and State" Principles Does Not Justify The Supreme Court's Seizure of Illicit Power

In my opinion, some of the principles developed under the "separation of church and state" doctrine and more specifically, the "purpose-effect-entanglement" test, are desirable public policy. For instance, I believe that public school children in state-run schools should not be forced to pray. However, I believe public school officials should be able to require a time of silence, which would permit silent prayer *or* quiet contemplation by the students on a voluntary basis. The U.S. Supreme Court disagrees. A statute allowing silent prayer *or* silent meditation has been struck down as unconstitutional. [18]

Even if some applications of the "separation of church and state" principle are wise, *that does not justify the Supreme Court's illegal seizure of power* to impose that principle without any democratic process whatsoever. The American people, or their elected representatives, should be able to vote on these issues in accordance with democratic processes, unless the actual language of the Establishment Clause applies.

As the U.S. Supreme Court itself has said in determining an act of Congress to be unconstitutional:

"Indeed, we also have observed only recently that 'the hydraulic pressure within each of the separate Branches *to exceed the outer limits of its power*, even *to accomplish desirable objectives*, must be *resisted*." [19]

In other words, a branch of the federal government *should not be permitted* to act outside the power to which it is limited under the U.S. Constitution. According to the Supreme Court itself, this is true even if the illegal action of that branch involves making a "*desirable*" law.

This principle should be applied to the U.S. Supreme Court. The Supreme Court "exceed[ed] the outer limits of its power" when it made and expanded constitutional law under the "separation of church and state" doctrine. Therefore the application of that doctrine "must be resisted," according to the Supreme Court itself.

If the Supreme Court is permitted to continue making constitutional law, America is no longer a democracy in areas the Supreme Court decides to act. We are under "the despotism of an oligarchy," as Thomas Jefferson warned. [20]

In view of these circumstances, Americans should "oblige" the federal courts to control themselves, as James Madison put it. [21] The only meaningful way to do that is to require Congress to apply the impeachment and removal procedures to judges who make constitutional law. That check will then be a "complete security," in Alexander Hamilton's words. [22]

The Ten Commandments Display Cases Which Are Currently Pending Before The U.S. Supreme Court: *Van Orden v. Perry* And *ACLU v. McCreary County*

As mentioned above, the U.S. Supreme Court is expected to decide appeals from two Court of Appeals cases during or soon after July 2005. Both of those cases involve Ten Commandments displays in government facilities. The oral argument for those two cases is presently scheduled to take place in the Supreme Court building on March 2, 2005.

In the first case, Van Orden v. Perry (2003), the Fifth Circuit Court of Appeals held a Ten Commandments display to be *constitutional* under the Establishment Clause. [23]

In the second case, ACLU of Kentucky v. McCreary County (2003), the Sixth Circuit Court of Appeals held various Ten Commandments displays to be *unconstitutional* under the Establishment Clause. [24]

The facts and reasoning of the <u>Van Orden</u> and <u>McCreary County</u> cases will be discussed briefly below. However, in view of the pending U.S. Supreme Court review of those cases, and the limited number of significant additional relevant issues, this book will not discuss these cases thoroughly.

The *Van Orden* Case

In <u>Van Orden</u>, the plaintiff sought an order of the federal court to remove a granite monument of the Ten Commandments displayed on the grounds of a 22-acre complex owned by the State of Texas. Both the U.S. District Court and the Fifth Circuit Court of Appeals found that the Ten Commandments monument *did not violate the Establishment Clause* of the First Amendment (as applied to the states through the Fourteenth Amendment).

Although the Court discussed many details concerning the Texas Ten Commandments monument, the key facts appeared to be the following:

1. The Ten Commandments monument had been *in place for approximately 42 years* before the lawsuit was brought;
2. The Ten Commandments monument was one of 17 monuments that were displayed on the Capitol grounds of the State of Texas which was designated as an *historical landmark*;
3. The Texas Capitol grounds had, in addition to the 17 monuments, plaques and seals depicting the *secular and religious history* of Texas;
4. The purpose of the Texas legislature in installing the monument was to recognize and commend the Fraternal Order of Eagles in its efforts to reduce juvenile delinquency; and
5. Texas had a consistent practice of honoring the contributions of donors to the state. [25]

In applying the "purpose-effect-entanglement" test, the <u>Van Orden</u> Court concluded there was a "secular purpose" for the monument, and the *effect* of the monument was *not* to advance or inhibit religion. The plaintiff did not argue that there was an inappropriate entanglement with religion (the third element of the "purpose-effect-entanglement" test).

The *McCreary County* Case

In the <u>McCreary County</u> case, the plaintiff challenged the displays of the Ten Commandments in both public schools *and* county courthouses.

After prior failed attempts to make displays that would satisfy the U.S. District Court, the final *courthouse displays* in McCreary had the following elements:

1. The *Ten Commandments*, The Declaration of Independence, the Mayflower Compact, the Bill of Rights, the Magna Carta, the National Motto, the Star Spangled Banner, Lady Justice, and the Preamble to the Kentucky Constitution; and
2. A description of the display items which stated, among other things, that the "display contains documents that played a significant role in the foundation of our system of law and government." The description also stated that "[t]he Ten Commandments have profoundly influenced the formation of Western legal thought and the formation of our country. That significance is clearly seen in the Declaration of Independence . . . ." [26]

The *public school displays* had an arrangement of items that was not different in any important way to the courthouse displays. The description, however, was different. The description said the items in the display "contribute to the educational foundations and moral character of students in our schools." The display items were also declared to be "valuable examples of documents that may instill qualities desirable of the students in our schools and have had historical significance in the development of this country." [27]

In its application of the "purpose-effect-entanglement" test, the Sixth Circuit Court first found that the displays had a *non-secular purpose* (regarding the first element of that test). The Court held that the Ten Commandments portion of the displays had religious elements. The Court further found that the Ten Commandments display was not combined with a secular message, such as an explanation of the connection between the Ten Commandments and American traditions or "an objective study of history, ethics or comparative religion." [28]

In addition, the Sixth Circuit Court held that the effect of the displays was to endorse religion (the second element of the "purpose-effect-entanglement" test). The primary reasons for the Court's conclusion was that the Ten Commandments stuck out "like a proverbial 'sore thumb' " as a religious item, in the context of the other items in the displays. Also, the Court concluded that the *coercive* contexts of courthouses and public schools enhanced the effect of an endorsement of religion. [29]

Both the courthouse and public school Ten Commandments displays were recently placed.

Eight Additional Court Of Appeals Decisions Regarding Ten Commandments Displays

There have been a number of other recent Court of Appeals decisions regarding Ten Commandment displays. The ACLU, and perhaps other similar organizations, are apparently engaging in a systematic effort to eliminate Ten Commandments displays, and other religions symbols, from government facilities.

In five of those decisions, the Ten Commandments

displays were held to be unconstitutional. Three of these display cases involved *newly placed* displays.[30] The fourth case related to a *future* intention to erect a Ten Commandments display. [31]

The fifth case involved a supposedly unconstitutional Ten Commandments display that had been in place since 1965. The display stood alone in a city park.[32] The Plattsmouth case is difficult to reconcile with the opposite result in the Van Orden case, where the Ten Commandments display had been in place a slightly longer time, namely 42 years. One other distinguishing fact in Van Orden that may influence the Supreme Court was that the Ten Commandments display was part of an historical landmark which had other historic displays. [33]

In three other Court of Appeals cases the Ten Commandments displays were found to be constitutional. The displays in those three cases had been in place for more than eighty years. [34]

It appears that the federal courts have now resorted to artificial distinctions concerning, for example, the age of the displays to distinguish between allowable and prohibited Ten Commandments displays. The federal courts seem to be making up new legal standards as time passes without any relationship to the actual language and history of the Establishment Clause.

All of the cases declaring a Ten Commandments display to be unconstitutional depend on the "separation of church and state" doctrine. Therefore, if the "separation of church and state" doctrine is found to be unconstitutional, as should happen, the legal bases for all of the cases which found the Ten Commandments displays to be unconstitutional will be eliminated.

CHAPTER 10

THE REASONS FOR THE ONLY MEANINGFUL POST-APPOINTMENT CONSTITUTIONAL CHECK ON JUDICIAL TYRANNY: IMPEACHMENT AND REMOVAL OF JUDGES FROM OFFICE

Barbara Lee was twenty-two years old and had achieved her long-desired independence. The previous June, Barbara had graduated from UCLA. She was now teaching U.S. history and Western Civilization classes at Jackson High School in the San Fernando Valley. It was a warm, sunny day in early October, typical for the Los Angeles area at that time of year.

"Hi, teach. Did my homework this time," said 18 year-old Robert Alton. Although the students spoke to Barbara almost like one of their peers, they respected her because she cared about them.

"That's great. Make that a habit, and you'll be glad you did. It will pay dividends for the rest of your life," quipped Barbara.

After the last class, Barbara drove to her apartment. As

usual, she immediately called her fiancé, Greg Park. "I love you," she said. "Love you, too," Greg returned. "I'll meet you at El Tostito in 45 minutes." "I'll miss you 'til then," she cooed.

Barbara sang love songs as she got ready. It was a wonderful evening. She felt like she was floating on air. When she returned to her apartment, she fell asleep singing again.

* * *

Barbara's father, John Lee, was at work when he had an unexpected visitor. In his office was detective Ken Alexander. John knew something was wrong. "I have some grim news. We believe your daughter, Barbara, has been murdered. We believe we know the identity of the killer and we will arrest him soon. We need you to identify her for us," said the detective pointing to an envelope he was carrying.

John could not hold back the tears. "What happened?" he asked. "She was engaged to be married this November."

"She was raped and murdered in her apartment. We have fingerprints that match those of a recently-released murderer and rapist. We have body fluid samples also. We have DNA records, in addition to the fingerprint patterns for that suspect. We have ordered a DNA report," assured the detective. "Can you identify this is a photograph of your daughter?"

John looked at the photograph of Barbara's bruised, bloody face and began sobbing uncontrollably. After a few minutes, he gathered himself as best he could. "That's her. Who could do something like that? How did he get out of prison?"

"The suspect was released because of a recent Supreme Court ruling. He originally had received a life sentence without any possibility of parole. But the Supreme Court ruled that any sentence longer than 30 years is cruel and unusual punishment. The suspect had been in prison for 34 years, and so he was released. If it is any consolation, we believe we will find him soon. Based on previous experience, he is not sophisticated at avoiding capture."

"I can't believe it," John muttered with his face in his hands.

About the Foregoing Hypothetical Story

The U.S. Supreme court has *not* determined that criminals that have been in prison more than 30 years for a single crime must be released. However, for practical purposes, the Supreme Court has the *power* to make such a ruling at some time in the future, without any means of changing such a law reasonably soon after the law is made.

The Eighth Amendment to the U.S. Constitution prohibits "cruel and unusual punishment" for convicted criminals. There is nothing in the way constitutional law is applied today to stop the Supreme Court from determining that any criminal sentence of greater than 30 years is "cruel and unusual punishment." If that happened, no criminal could be imprisoned for more than 30 years for any crime no matter what laws the elected representatives of the American people enacted.

Furthermore, if the Supreme Court made such a rule of constitutional law, the only meaningful penalty the Supreme Court justices could suffer (other than public disapproval) would be impeachment and removal from office by Congress. Such a law could be corrected by a democratically-ratified constitutional amendment, but that would take several years.

Many legal experts, including the Supreme Court itself, claim that impeachment and removal by Congress should *never* be used against a judge who illegally makes constitutional law. These people believe that no federal judges should ever be removed from office because of a judicial decision made by that judge, no matter how offensive the decision is to the American people.

As explained below, the concept of unchecked governmental power in the hands of the Supreme Court (or any other small group of people) is very dangerous. In spite of this, many legal experts believe that unchecked judicial power is and should be the law.

The language of the Constitution itself, as well as the writings of the framers of the Constitution do not support that dangerous view. The framers believed that no persons could be trusted with unchecked governmental power, no matter how strong their characters may be. They also believed that impeachment and removal is the appropriate check on the federal judiciary when the judiciary engages in law-making.

The Founders Believed That Even People Of Good Character Cannot Be Trusted With Unchecked Governmental Powers

Those who oppose any meaningful inter-branch check on the federal judiciary sometimes argue that the way to ensure that judges do not abuse their power is for the President to appoint, in the first instance, judges of good character. If the President appoints only judges of good character, so the argument goes, judges will not exceed their power.

The founders, and even the U.S. Supreme Court itself, have expressed principles that strongly refute this argument. Governmental power is very seductive. The most decent people can and do succumb to the availability of illicit governmental power.

David Mayer in his book, *The Constitutional Thought of Thomas Jefferson*, has characterized the views of Thomas Jefferson on that subject as follows:

"*Jefferson*. . . suspected that such an assumption-that the Supreme Court knew what was right for the nation-came too perilously close to 'playing God.' He. . . *saw all men-regardless of their character and circumstances-as inherently susceptible to the corruptions of power* and therefore *denied the notion of . . . trust and confidence in any public officeholders.* 'We shall all become wolves,' Jefferson once warned; *no man can be trusted with the government of others.*" [1]

Thomas Jefferson thus rejected the good character argument because he understood, as he put it, "the influence of interest on the mind of man, and how consciously his judgment is warped by that influence." [2] Jefferson believed that no person can be trusted with governmental power that is not counter-balanced (i.e., checked) by governmental power under the control of other persons.

James Madison had a similar view of the role of human nature in government:

"But what is government itself but the greatest of all reflections on human nature? If men were angels, no government would be necessary. *If angels were to govern men, neither external or internal controls on government would be necessary.* In framing a government which is to be administered by men over men, the great difficulty lies in this: *you must* first enable the government to control the governed; and in the next place *oblige it [the government] to control itself. A dependence on the people is, no doubt, the primary control on the government; but experience has taught mankind the necessity of auxiliary precautions.*" [3]

Thus, Madison believed that government officials needed to be controlled by the people first, and also by additional checks within the government. As Madison put it, the government must be "obliged[d] . . . to control itself." The American people have no direct control through elections over the federal judiciary, after judges are appointed to office. The *only* effective means of "oblig[ing]" the federal judiciary "to control itself" is held by Congress, through the impeachment and removal process. The impeachment power is a significant deterrent against judicial law-making, *if* it is exercised by Congress.

As mentioned above, the U.S. Supreme Court itself has expressed similar sentiments when overturning an act of Congress:

> "Indeed, we have observed only recently that the *'hydraulic pressure inherent within each of the separate branches to exceed the outer limits of its power*, even to accomplish desirable objectives, must be resisted.' " [4]

Thus, the Supreme Court itself admits that federal government officials, which includes the members of the U.S. Supreme Court, cannot be trusted to control themselves by voluntarily refraining from "exceed[ing] the outer limits of their power." Government officials "must be resisted" through checks by one of the other branches or by the American people, and preferably both.

To sum it up, federal judges who think their views on particular issues are best for everyone else *do* give in to the temptation of imposing their views on other Americans, without any democratic process. That is an abuse of power that must be addressed. If not, democracy in America may become a relic of the past. There is only one meaningful way to remedy the abuse of political power by judges after they are appointed to office; that remedy is impeachment and removal by Congress.

The "Evolutionary" Theory Of Constitutional Analysis Is A Prescription For Judge-Made Constitutional Amendments

Those Americans who support judicially-created changes to the U.S. Constitution argue that the Constitution is a "living" or "organic" document. In other words, the provisions of the Constitution should *evolve* over time, without any democratic approval process.

According to these people, the U.S. Constitution was created only for eighteenth century society. These Americans believe that judges need to have the power to read into the Constitution meanings that are different from what was originally intended, in order to adapt to changing circumstances and values in society.

This "evolutionary" or "living document" theory of constitutional interpretation gives federal judges the power to bypass democratic processes for making constitutional amendments. That idea opposes the framers' distrust of people who have unchecked governmental power. It is a prescription for tyranny.

Former Chief Justice Earl Warren of the U.S. Supreme Court adhered to the "evolutionary" theory of constitutional analysis. Chief Justice Warren claimed that the Constitution needs to have a meaning that reflects "the *evolving standards of decency* that mark the progress of a maturing society." [5]

Another U.S. Supreme Court justice, William Brennan, Jr., stated it this way: "I approached my responsibility of interpreting it [i.e., the Constitution] as a 20th century American . . . for the genius of the Constitution rests not in any static meaning it may have had in a world dead and gone but in its *evolving* character." [6]

The leading proponent of the "living" document or

"evolutionary" theory of constitutional analysis today is Professor Lawrence Tribe of Harvard Law School. In his book, *God Save This Honorable Court*, Tribe has stated as follows:

> "Should the peculiar opinion held, and the particular applications envisioned, by men who have been dead for two centuries *always* trump *contemporary insights* into what the *living Constitution* means and *ought to mean*?" [7]

From the written context of this rhetorical question, it is obvious that Professor Tribe's answer is a resounding "no." However, if one evaluates the situation, the proper answer is closer to "yes" than "no." Some similar quotes from Professor Tribe's book are discussed below.

What is Professor Tribe saying when he refers to "contemporary insights into what the living Constitution means and ought to mean?" The "contemporary insights" are those of a few current judges on the U.S. Supreme Court. The "living Constitution" refers to constitutional principles that can be shaped to fit the "contemporary insights" of these judges. The Constitution will then mean what these judges think it "ought to mean."

The "men who have been dead for two centuries" were democratically selected representatives of the American people, unlike federal judges. Furthermore, the Constitution had to be democratically ratified by the American people through their state governments, unlike the opinions of the U.S. Supreme Court.

The first response to Professor Tribe's rhetorical question is that the Constitution's provisions are *timeless principles* that are very relevant today. For example, the "freedom of speech" in the First Amendment is repeatedly exercised by Americans today, when they engage in political discourse that is against the desires of those in powerful political positions. This book is an example.

The second response is that allowing judges to inject their "contemporary insights" into what the constitutional principles "ought to mean" is a very dangerous idea. It gives judges the power to bypass democracy and make constitutional law based on their own personal views. That notion is far more dangerous than any risk that the timeless principles of the Constitution may become outdated.

The Constitution can and should be changed, if necessary, only by a democratic process. It is better and fairer for the people of America to rule themselves through democratic processes than it is for a few judges to rule the American people through unchecked judicial power.

Later in his discussion, Professor Tribe stated it this way:

> "The *Supreme Court* just *cannot avoid the painful duty* of exercising judgment so as to give concrete meaning to the *fluid Constitution*, because the constitutional rules and precepts that it is charged with administering *lack that certainty* which permits anything resembling automatic application." [8]

The concept of a "fluid Constitution" that "lack[s] . . . certainty" allows the Supreme Court to shape constitutional law in its own image. What does "fluid" do? It takes the shape of its container. What is the container here? It is the U.S. Supreme Court.

The principles in the Constitution, when understood in their historical context, are very relevant today and do not "lack . . . certainty" any more than most other laws. Those constitutional principles are timeless and were *derived from many centuries of bitter human experience*. Constitutional principles should *always* be applied in light of their actual language and their historical context, in order to prevent a few judges from imposing their will on the American people. Such tyranny by a few people (e.g., judges) is precisely what our Constitution's timeless principles were designed to prevent.

Tribe's fear that "a Constitution frozen in eighteenth-century ice would soon become obsolete," is unfounded.[9] The principles in the actual language of the Constitution are not rigid and unfair for today's society, as Professor Tribe apparently believes. Furthermore, assuming for the sake of argument a constitutional principle lacks current relevance in some respect, Professor Tribe's approach of giving judges the power to inject their view of what that constitutional principle "ought to mean" is a much bigger problem. Professor Tribe's approach empowers the tyranny of a few people.

If the existing principles in the actual language of the U.S. Constitution are inadequate, *according to the American people*, the Constitution can be amended by the democratic process provided for in Article V. As an alternative resolution, Congress or state legislators can enact laws through the usual *democratic* processes to provide for new rights that are appropriate. Congress and state legislators can do this by a simple majority vote. If those new laws are later found to be inappropriate, they can be repealed or changed by legislators, unlike constitutional principles created by the U.S. Supreme Court. The Supreme Court's constitutional amendments based on the personal views of a few people are almost permanent.

Lest the reader doubt that my characterization of Professor Tribe's views is correct, he summed up his discussion with the following statement:

> "[T]here is simply no getting around the fact that whenever the *Supreme Court* turns to the Constitution, it *must inject a lot of substantive meaning*

into the words and the structure, and thus the overall message, of that majestic but *incomplete document.*" **10**

Thus, Professor Tribe believes the Supreme Court must have substantial discretion to shape the Constitution and "inject" its own views of what the Constitution "ought to mean" into our nation's constitutional law. Professor Tribe is considered by many to be the top American scholar of constitutional law. His writings have been relied upon by U.S. Supreme Court justices in their opinions. That is a rarity for an academician such as Professor Tribe.

The bottom line is that Professor Tribe, some federal judges, and others with similar views *do not trust the American people* to do what is fair and reasonable. However, *they do trust a few judges* on the U.S. Supreme Court. Like the framers of the Constitution, I do not trust a few men and women to rule over the rest of us. Although it is possible for a democratic majority to be oppressive, it is much more likely that a few judges will be oppressive. I believe the vast majority of Americans agree with that view. Those who think they know what is good for the rest of us do not agree.

The "Evolutionary" Theory Of Constitutional Analysis Is Very Dangerous

I believe that persons with a view point similar to that of Professor Tribe would agree with the positions taken in this book against judge-made constitutional law, if they strongly disagreed with what the U.S. Supreme Court was injecting into constitutional principles. In other words, if those same people thought the Supreme Court was using its effective immunity from democratic processes to impose oppressive constitutional principles on the American people, I believe that they would support impeachment and removal of judges who engage in such practices.

However, whether one agrees with what judges are doing should *not* determine whether those judges are allowed to exceed their power. As the Supreme Court itself has said, any branch of the federal government that exceeds its power "must be resisted," even if what it is doing is "desirable." [11] Allowing the abuse of power creates the kind of power vacuum that has resulted in great evils in human history, including unintended ones.

The "living" document or "evolutionary" theory of constitutional analysis is a recipe for judge-made constitutional law. That notion, which is reflected in numerous Supreme Court opinions, is a threat to democracy in America.

I will refer to the hypothetical story at the beginning of this chapter to make the point in a different way. If the "evolutionary" theory of constitutional analysis was the law, what keeps the U.S. Supreme Court from requiring the release from prison of murderers who have served more than thirty years in prison? The thirty-year limit on a prison sentence for killers would be in accord with the Supreme Court's view of the "current standards of decency."

The answer to the question is that nothing presently prevents the Supreme Court from releasing such murderers except the Supreme Court's voluntary self-restraint. There is no higher authority to which the American people can appeal, and no meaningful counter-balance in the federal government, other than removal from office by Congress through impeachment procedures.

Such removal would not immediately change the law, however. A constitutional amendment could be ratified to correct the problem, but that would take several years. It would also require approval of three-quarters of the states. Judges should not be able to permanently change the Constitution if only *slightly* more than one-quarter of the states agree with the U.S. Supreme Court, and almost three-quarters of the states disagree. But that is the result that the "evolutionary" theory of constitutional analysis provides. That theory is a very dangerous and oppressive idea that should be eliminated from American law.

Those That Are Against Impeachment And Removal Of Federal Judges Who Abuse The "Evolutionary" Theory Of Constitutional Analysis Are Wrong

There are several arguments that support exercising the impeachment/removal power to remove judges who make constitutional law, and that undermine an unchecked power to inject meaning into an "evolutionary" Constitution.

First, almost everyone agrees that the U.S. Constitution and the Bill of Rights guarantee certain rights to *all* Americans, whether or not they are in a minority group. *Any judge who refuses to protect the existing, democratically-ratified constitutional rights of individuals (including those in a minority group) should be impeached and removed from office for that reason.* However, judges should not be able to create or modify constitutional rights in their own image. Creation or modification of constitutional principles is, and should be, permitted only by a democratic process. If judges change the Constitution unilaterally, they should be candidates for removal from office by Congress.

A second response to those against impeachment of judges who make constitutional law is that the most serious consequence that is possible from impeachment procedures is the removal and exclusion from office of a particular judge. The judge cannot be sent to jail, unless he or she is convicted of a crime in a separate judicial trial. Any conviction for separate criminal behavior would have to occur in the courts, not in Congress. Removal from of judicial office is a mild punishment for usurping governmental power. Members of Congress and the President who have *not* violated the Constitution by exceeding their power are frequently removed from office through elections.

A third response is that impeachment and removal of a judge does not change the law. Constitutional law would have to be corrected by subsequent judicial decisions. Therefore, by applying impeachment/removal procedures to remove a judge from office, Congress would not be dictating constitutional law, as unelected judges do today.

Fourth, it takes a substantial amount of political will to impeach and remove a federal judge, as is demonstrated by the near non-existence of impeachments in U.S. history. A judicial decision, or a series of decisions, would have to be a serious political power grab for the actual removal of a judge to occur. An impeachment trial in Congress is a highly public event and so would be hotly debated in the public forum. Therefore, if most Americans believed removal would be unjust, removal would very likely not occur. If most Americans believe a judge should be removed from office for judicial law-making, it should occur. To reiterate, the President and members of Congress are frequently removed from office through elections.

Fifth, and most importantly, is it fair and reasonable for the votes of a few judges to make the laws that control more than a hundred million Americans? The answer is obvious. As explained above, *no men or women can be trusted with the government of others*.

I can think of numerous examples in human history where domination by a minority of people in a society resulted in despicable evils such as genocide. Hitler's Germany, Stalinist Russia and Mao Tse Tung's China are three examples. I can think of *no* examples of such despicable evils perpetrated by a ruling democratic majority of the people in any society. The founders of the U.S. Constitution repeatedly expressed a similar sentiment because of the experience from recorded European history as of 1776. Although judges do not have the power to directly use force that dictators have had, if they can engage in unchecked anti-democratic law-making, they can do many oppressive things.

Excluding the abortion issue, the most egregious example of oppression by a democratic majority in world history, that I can think of, is the enforcement of slavery. However, many non-democratic societies ruled by a few people have also enforced slavery. America now has an express constitutional amendment against that evil practice which was democratically ratified. Rule by a few people is clearly worse than rule by a majority of the people.

The actual line between legitimate application of an express constitutional provision and creating a new provision (i.e., law-making) is sometimes difficult to identify. However, that is a problem in most areas of the law, including criminal law. Since "crossing the line" creates at most a risk of impeachment and removal from office by a two-thirds vote in the Senate, the principle of impeaching judges for exceeding their constitutional power is not a drastic remedy. It will probably only deter judges from creating new constitutional principles in situations in which they should be deterred. In fact, many situations where deterrence is appropriate will likely not result in sufficient political will for impeachment and/or removal. That has been universally true to this point in American history. No U.S. judge has yet been removed from office for illegally amending the Constitution.

The Detractors Of Any Check On Judicial Power In Order To Maintain "Judicial Independence" Are Also Wrong

The proponents of the "evolutionary" theory of constitutional construction argue that judges should be able to go beyond the actual language and history of the Constitution to create principles not previously known, in order to protect minorities from oppression by the majority in a democratic society. Many of the same people argue against impeachment and removal of federal judges from office who make constitutional law. They argue that, if judges are threatened with removal from office, judges will be deterred from protecting the constitutional rights of minorities and individuals.

In other words, the people who are against exercising any check on the power of the judiciary argue that judges need to be "independent" so they can protect minorities and individuals in society against the "tyranny of the majority." However, as mentioned above, *the theoretical possibility of a tyranny of the majority does not justify the more oppressive tyranny of a few judges.* In fact, our Constitution's democratically-ratified constitutional rights, as applied according to their language and historical context, *protect against a tyranny of the majority.*

Judges should be protected from impeachment or removal if they protect individuals or groups of people by applying democratically-ratified constitutional rights. However, if judges create new constitutional rights, they are seizing power and taking self-government away from the American people. Such judges appropriately expose themselves to the risk of being removed from office.

Federal judges will remain in office during "good [b]ehavior," as the Constitution states. It is not "good [b]ehavior" for a judge to take power that the Constitution does not give him or her. As long as a judge stays within the limits of his or her power, and applies true constitutional liberties and other laws, there is no basis for removal (absent, for example, criminal behavior). On the other hand, if a judge goes outside his or her power and enacts what is in effect a constitutional amendment, he or she has abused his or her power and is properly at risk of being removed from office.

Being a judge is a privilege given by the American

people, not a judge's right. As things presently stand, federal judges have been impeached and removed by Congress so infrequently that judges do not consider such a prospect to be a remotely serious risk.

The only way Congress will impeach and remove these judges is if the American people *demand* that Congress do that. The opposition would be fierce by Americans who are quite happy with the new constitutional laws being imposed by the courts today. Many of these people are very politically active. It is time that the American people say "no more" to judicial power grabbing. If we do not fight for our constitutional protections and rights, including the right to vote for those who make our laws, we may lose them.

The January 1, 2005 Report On The Federal Judiciary Wrongly Argues That Federal Judges Should Never Be Impeached And Removed Due To Their Judicial Decisions

On January 1, 2005, Chief Supreme Court Justice William Rehnquist issued the "2004 Year-End Report on the Federal Judiciary." The longest section of that report was entitled "Criticism of Judges Based on Judicial Acts." In that section, the Chief Justice argued that "Congress' authority to impeach and remove judges should not extend to decisions from the bench." [12]

The basis for that argument was, according to the Chief Justice, "established nearly 200 years ago" when Congress impeached Supreme Court Justice Samuel B. Chase, but did not remove him from office. The Chief Justice stated as follows:

"[T]he Senate's failure to convict him [i.e., Supreme Court Justice Samuel B. Chase] represented a judgment that impeachment should not be used to remove a judge for conduct in the exercise of his judicial duties. The political precedent set by Chase's acquittal has governed the use of impeachment to remove federal judges from that day to this: a judge's *judicial acts* may not serve as a basis for impeachment. Any other rule would *destroy judicial independence* – instead of trying to apply the law fairly, regardless of public opinion, judges would be concerned about inflaming any group that might be able to muster the votes in Congress to impeach and convict them." [13]

The first response to this argument is that any position of a Supreme Court justice about whether federal judges should be impeached and removed from office involves an *inherent conflict of interest*. In other words, the self-interest of the Chief Justice to protect himself and his colleagues from impeachment and removal is obvious. The Chief Justice has to work with the other Supreme Court justices on a daily basis. Some of them are probably his close friends. The Chief Justice's conflict of interest is thus quite understandable, and perhaps even praise-worthy. However, when it comes to something as important as the power to determine how our nation's constitutional laws are to be applied, and potentially illegally made, that conflict of interest is a *strong negative factor*, not a favorable one.

The second response is that Samuel Chase *was impeached* by Congress. Therefore, that early Congress thought that Justice Samuel Chase's judicial decisions were potentially a basis for impeachment and removal.

Furthermore, there are plausible reasons why the Senate, after a trial, did not vote by a two-thirds "super majority" to remove Justice Chase from office other than that "impeachment should not be used to remove a judge for conduct in the exercise of his judicial duties." One of those potential reasons was that Justice Chase's specific behavior was not serious enough to justify removal (although it was clearly enough to warrant impeachment by the House of Representatives).

In addition, many legal historians believe that Justice Chase was not removed by the Senate because the leader of the Senate trial against Justice Chase offended other Senators. As stated by late Professor Raoul Berger of Harvard Law School regarding Justice Chase's trial in the Senate:

> "Most students of the era consider that conviction [of Justice Chase] failed of a two-thirds vote because the inept, acid-tongued manager of the impeachment, JOHN RANDOLPH, had alienated many Republicans, as well as Federalists." [14]

Another response to the Chief Justice's Annual Report is that impeachment and removal of a federal judge for engaging in judicial law-making would *not* "destroy judicial independence" that is *appropriately* exercised. When a judge applies democratically-ratified constitutional amendments, that judge cannot be legitimately impeached and removed from office for his or her judicial decisions. Such a judge's "independence" should be maintained. However, when a judge violates the Constitution's "separation of powers" doctrine by seizing law-making power, that judge's "judicial independence" should be taken away. Such a judge is usurping legislative (not judicial) power and is thus violating the Constitution. Most principles in the U.S. Constitution were designed to *prevent such concentrations of governmental power* under the control of a few people.

For the foregoing reasons, the impeachment and removal of federal judges who engage in law-making is entirely *consistent* with the *appropriate* kind of "judicial independence" contemplated by the founders. Alexander

Hamilton put it this way:

> "The precautions for their (i.e., federal judges')
> responsibility are comprised in the article respecting
> *impeachments*. They are liable to be impeached for
> malconduct by the House of Representatives and
> tried by the Senate; and, if convicted, may be
> dismissed from office and disqualified for holding
> any other. This is the only provision on the point
> which is *consistent with the necessary independence
> of the judicial character*, and is the only one which
> we find in our own Constitution in respect to our
> own judges." [15]

In the next chapter, it is explained how the founders
unquestionably considered judicial law-making to be an
appropriate basis for impeachment and removal of federal
judges under the U.S. Constitution. Therefore, Chief Justice
Rehnquist's view that federal judges should *never* be
impeached and removed from office because of a judicial
decision in order to preserve "judicial independence," is
contrary to the views of the founders of our Constitution.

CHAPTER 11

THE MECHANISMS AND STANDARDS FOR THE ONLY MEANINGFUL POST-APPOINTMENT CONSTITUTIONAL CHECK ON JUDICIAL TYRANNY: IMPEACHMENT AND REMOVAL OF JUDGES FROM OFFICE

⊣⇒⇒⊢

This chapter will explain the constitutional provisions and the founders' principles related to impeachment and removal of federal judges from office. Also discussed below are the reasons that impeachment and removal of federal judges are more politically feasible now than ever before in American history.

The Potential Life-Time Term In Office Of A Federal Judge

The constitutional provisions regarding the term in office of federal judges will be discussed here. By way of reminder, federal judges are appointed to their positions by the President, with the consent of the Senate. They are not elected by the American people. Furthermore, federal judges are not subject to re-election after they are appointed.

The constitutional provision that governs the term of office for federal judges is found in Article III, Section I, of the Constitution, which states:

> "The Judges, both of the supreme and inferior Courts, shall hold their offices *during good Behavior. . .*" [1]

Thus, after their appointment, federal judges remain in office for the rest of their lives as long as they engage in "good [b]ehavior," and do not retire.

When federal judges begin their tenure in office, they are required to promise under oath or affirmation to support the Constitution. The relevant provision is found in Article VI, Clause 3 of the Constitution as follows:

> "[A]ll *judicial officers*, both of the United States and the several States, shall be *bound by Oath or affirmation, to support this Constitution...* [2]

As explained above in Chapters Three and Four, judicial officers are not permitted by the Constitution to make new laws, including constitutional amendments. Only Congress is permitted to make federal laws. As explained in Chapter Five, only Congress in combination with elected state representatives are permitted to make constitutional amendments. Therefore, if judges make new laws, such as constitutional amendments, they have violated their oath to uphold the Constitution. A judge's violation of his or her oath of office is clearly not "good [b]ehavior." Thus, if a federal judge makes new law, he or she can properly be removed from office because his or her tenure lasts only during the judge's "good [b]ehavior."

Impeachment And Removal Of Federal Judges From Office

As mentioned above, the Constitution provides a mechanism to remove a federal judge. To summarize, a federal judge can be "impeached" by the House of Representatives. The Senate then holds a trial and decides by a *two-thirds* majority whether the judge should be *removed* from office.

As the Constitution provides, the *"House* of Representatives... shall have the sole Power of *impeachment."* [3] Moreover, "[t]he *Senate* shall have the sole Power to *try all impeachments."* [4] Finally, "no Person shall be convicted [in the Senate after impeachment] without the Concurrence of *two thirds* of the Members present." [5]

In addition to being subject to removal from office for failing to maintain "good behavior," the Constitution provides that judges are to be removed from office for impeachment and conviction in the Senate of treason, bribery, or "[h]igh [c]rimes and [m]isdemeanors." This basis for impeachment and removal is set forth in Article II, Section 4 as follows:

> "The President, Vice President and *all civil officers* of the United States, shall be removed from Office on Impeachment for, and Conviction of, Treason, Bribery, or other *High Crimes and Misdemeanors."* [6]

The terms "High Crimes and Misdemeanors" include offenses against the State (i.e., the government). [7] The violation of a judge's oath of office to support the Constitution by illegally making constitutional law is an impeachable offense against the federal government (i.e., the "State"). Therefore, such an act exposes a judge to impeachment and removal.

Some argue that only judges that have committed indictable crimes can be impeached. However, as Professor

Berger of Harvard Law School stated:

"[No] statute declared 'abuse of power,' 'neglect of duty,' or 'subversion of the Constitution' to be criminal, yet the Founders unquestionably regarded these as impeachable offenses." [8]

For a federal judge to violate the Constitution is clearly an "abuse of power" and a "subversion of the Constitution." Therefore, when a federal judge makes constitutional law, the judge exposes himself or herself to potential impeachment and removal.

Alexander Hamilton made statements in the *Federalist Papers* that support Professor Berger's view:

"The subjects of its [i.e., the Senate's] jurisdiction [concerning 'the trial of *impeachments*'] are those offenses which proceed from the misconduct of public men, or in other words, from the *abuse or violation of some public trust*. They are of a nature which may with peculiar propriety be denominated POLITICAL, as *they relate chiefly to injuries done to the society itself*. The prosecution of them, for this reason, will seldom fail to agitate the passions of the whole community, and to divide it into parties more or less friendly or inimical to the accused." [9]

Thus, the concept of a judge's "abuse of power" being a basis for impeachment and removal is in the founders' writings.

The Founders Thought That Impeachment And Removal Was Appropriate For Judges Who Make Law

The writings of the framers of the Constitution support

applying the impeachment and removal procedures to federal judges that exceed their power by making constitutional law. Both James Madison and Alexander Hamilton expressed their beliefs in the *Federalist Papers* that the impeachment and removal procedures were an appropriate check against judges that usurp the power to make federal law.

In the *Federalist Papers*, No. 47, Madison discussed the dangers of one of the three branches exercising the power of one of the other branches. Madison wrote specifically about the judicial branch exercising the legislative (i.e., law-making) power. Quoting the political philosopher, Montesquieu, Madison said:

> " 'Were the power of judging joined with the legislative, the life and liberty of the subject would be exposed to arbitrary control, for *the judge* **would then be** *the legislator.*' " [10]

In the same discussion, Madison claimed that, although the functions of the three branches are separate and distinct, the branches check one another. He specifically referred to Congress' impeachment/removal power over judges as one of those checks:

> "The entire legislature [i.e., Congress] can perform no judiciary act, though by the joint act of two of its branches [i.e., the House and the Senate] *the judges may be removed* from their offices . . . ." [11]

Thus, in discussing the dangers of one branch (e.g., the judiciary) exercising the law-making power of another branch (e.g., the Congress), Madison raised the issue of the impeachment/removal of judges, a power held by the two legislative bodies of Congress.

Alexander Hamilton also addressed the issue in the

Federalist Papers, No. 81. In discussing the danger of encroachments of the judiciary on the power of Congress to make law, he said that the impeachment/removal procedures were a *"complete security"* against such a power grab. He also incorrectly stated that the danger of such encroachments was a "phantom," due to the weakness of the judicial branch. His analysis was the following:

"It may in the last place be observed that the supposed danger of *judiciary encroachments on the legislative authority* which has been upon many occasions reiterated is in reality a phantom. Particular misconstructions and contraventions of the will of the legislature may now and then happen; but they can never be so extensive as to amount to an inconvenience, or in any sensible degree to affect the order of the political system. This may be inferred with certainty from the general nature of the judicial power, from the objects to which it relates, from the manner in which it is exercised, from its comparative weakness, and from its total incapacity to support its usurpations by force. And the inference is greatly fortified by the consideration of *the important constitutional check* which *the power of instituting* **impeachments** in one part of the legislative body, and of determining upon them in the other, would give to that body *upon the members of the judicial department. This is alone a complete security*. There never can be danger that the *judges*, by a series of deliberate *usurpations on the authority of the legislature*, would hazard the united resentment of the body entrusted with it, while this body was possessed of the means of punishing their presumption by *degrading them from their stations*. While this ought to remove all apprehensions on the subject it affords, at the same time, *a cogent argument for constituting the Senate a court for the **trial of impeachments**.*" [12]

Hamilton's prediction that federal judges would never "affect the order of the political system" through "judiciary encroachments on the legislative authority" due to the weakness of the judicial branch was wrong. However, he went on to say there is a "complete" remedy in the Constitution if that situation arises, namely impeachment and removal of judges by Congress.

The U.S. Supreme Court itself has also emphasized the importance of inter-branch checks in the federal government. In fact, the U.S. Supreme Court has expressed the belief that each branch should be checked by *both* of the other branches:

"The idea and the promise [of the Constitution] were that when the people delegate some degree of control to a remote central authority, *one branch of government ought not possess the power to shape their destiny without a sufficient check from the other two.*" [13]

After a judge is appointed to office, the only meaningful check on the federal judiciary from either of the other branches of the federal government is the impeachment/removal power of Congress. The President has no power to remove or otherwise stop previously appointed federal judges from making law.

It is thus the sole responsibility of Congress to protect the American people from judicial power-grabbing by removing culpable judges from office. That is a responsibility Congress has *never* exercised in more than two hundred years of American history, to remove a judge from office.

Although Congress has removed a few judges from office, it has never done so for unconstitutional law-making.

The Economic Consequences For A Removed Judge Are Mild And Removal Would Not Harm America

The punishment for conviction in an impeachment trial is *limited to* removal from federal office and exclusion from future federal governmental positions. The relevant constitutional provision is found in Article I, Section 3, Clause 7. It states as follows:

> "Judgment in cases of impeachment *shall not extend further* than to *removal from office*, and *disqualification to hold* and enjoy *any Office* of honor, Trust or Profit under United States: but the Party convicted shall nevertheless be liable and subject to Indictment, Trial and Judgment and Punishment, according to law." [14]

Therefore, under the express provisions of the Constitution, the only punishment for any impeachment conviction is removal and disqualification from office. A removed judge will not go to jail or have to pay a fine, unless independently tried and convicted in a court of law for a separate criminal offense.

The reader should not be concerned about any adverse economic effect on a removed judge. If removed, the judge will likely be entitled to a government pension. Supreme Court justices, for example, are typically well beyond the usual retirement age.

Any Supreme Court or Court of Appeals judge who is removed from office for making law is also likely to be hired, if the judge desires, by prominent law firms at very high consulting fees, probably at a rate of $400 to $800 per hour. Why? Because the removed judge would have intimate knowledge of the patterns and preferences of the other judges in the important court of which he or she was a member. Powerful and wealthy clients of national law firms would be willing to pay substantial sums for such information.

Any removed federal court judge, especially U.S. District Court judges, would likely, if the judge desired, be hired as a private arbitrator or mediator of business disputes. Judges' experience in presiding over court trials would likely give them this kind of opportunity. Such persons are usually paid between $250 and $500 per hour for their services.

Other lucrative pursuits would also likely be available to a removed federal judge. Former judges may return to practicing law. Former judges are also often paid to speak at seminars for lawyers. Moreover, if a judge committed a serious enough breach of the Constitution to be removed by Congress, he or she would probably have many political supporters who would pay to hear that person speak at dinners and the like. Furthermore, such judges could write books about their experiences and about law. These are only a few of the profitable pursuits that may be available to a removed federal judge.

The bottom line is that a removed federal judge would probably do better economically after removal from office than before removal. Such judges would, however, not be permitted to exercise the powers of their former judicial office. Such a remedy for acting outside the judicial power in violation of the Constitution is both mild and justified.

Nor would America be significantly harmed if the experience of a removed just is lost from public service. There are no judges in America that are indispensable, including U.S. Supreme Court justices. There are many people that are highly qualified to replace any removed judge.

In conclusion, the consequences of removing a judge from office are not drastic. The harm caused by a judge that exceeds his or her judicial power is a much more serious consequence than impeachment and removal of that judge from office. Other federal government office holders, such as members of Congress or Presidents, are often removed from office through elections. If a judge abuses his or her power by injecting himself or herself into the political realm of law-making, removal from office is appropriate.

Impeachment And Removal Of Federal Judges Is Presently More Politically Feasible Then Ever Before In American History

Many experts who would support removal of federal judges for engaging in judicial law-making do not believe that impeachment and removal of such judges is politically feasible. In my view, that possibility is more likely today than ever before in American history.

There are three reasons for my view of the current political climate. First, there is an extensive record in judicial opinions which evidences substantial changes in constitutional law created by current federal judges without support in the actual language or history of the Constitution. Second, the concern of the American people about overreaching court decisions has never been as high as it is today. Nor have court decisions previously affected the outcome of a national election as they did in the November 2004 presidential election. Third, the make-up of Congress has not been as likely to favor impeachment and removal of federal judges during the past sixty or more years, as it is today.

As mentioned above, in 1805, Supreme Court Justice Samuel B. Chase was impeached by the House of Representatives, but not removed by the Senate. At that time, the federal courts were extremely limited in their application of federal law, unlike today. Therefore, at that time, there was no record of repeated changes to the Constitution, and the American public was not nearly as concerned about the federal judiciary as it is today.

Other unsuccessful impeachment efforts have been more recently tried by some Americans against Chief Supreme Court Justice Earl Warren and Supreme Court Justice, William O. Douglas during the 1960's and the 1970's, respectively. Those efforts were never seriously enough considered by Congress for an impeachment vote to even take place in the House. However, the make-up of Congress during those decades was much less likely to support removal of judges for engaging in judicial law-making than it is today. Furthermore, the American people were less informed about, and less concerned about, judicial law-making than they are now.

In any event, the issue of judicial law-making is too important to ignore, no matter what the chances of successful impeachment and removal are. The mere debate of the issue on a national scale may deter some federal judges from usurping illicit judicial power. It may also increase the likelihood that federal politicians will appoint and confirm federal judges who will in fact refrain from taking the right of self-government away from the American people.

CHAPTER 12

WHAT CAN BE DONE ABOUT JUDICIAL TYRANNY

What practical things can Americans do to stop the expansion of judicial tyranny? Based on the rarity of impeachment proceedings involving judges during more than two hundred years of American history, it is an extremely difficult task to motivate the House of Representatives to impeach a federal judge for any reason, including judicial law-making. It is an even more difficult task to motivate the Senate to conduct a trial and vote by a two-thirds majority to remove a federal judge. However, such a course of action *will* be seriously considered by Congress if Americans are politically active in demanding it.

Many political movements have been very small and ineffective in their beginnings but later became politically powerful because their supporters kept fighting for their causes. Examples of such movements are the feminist movement, and more recently the gay rights movement. These political movements have gained influence because of their vigor and persistence, not because of their numbers of adherents.

Many Americans who would support impeaching and

removing from office federal judges who engage in judicial law-making do not believe that such a remedy is likely in the U.S. Congress. As mentioned above, past efforts to impeach U.S. Supreme Court justices for that reason have not stirred any significant interest in Congress. However, conditions are different now than ever before in American history. The number of Americans who oppose judicial law-making is far greater than the number of adherents to many successful American political movements. I believe that those of us who oppose judicial law-making need to rise up and fight for our political freedoms. If we do that, we will probably be successful in at least substantially reducing the practice of judicial law-making. A two-thirds vote in the Senate is achievable.

What Can Be Done To Cause Congress To Consider Removal Of Law-Making Judges From Office

Of course, the most important response to judicial law-making is that the reader vote in every election. If Americans do not exercise their right to vote, the right to vote on important issues will probably continue to erode in America. The choice of candidates may not be the best. However, if one candidate is better than another, I believe Americans should almost always vote for the best alternative. Otherwise, oppressive laws are likely to be created in both Congress and the courts.

The reader should also keep informed about, as well as provide both financial and voting support for, politicians that are investigating or seeking impeachment of an appropriate federal judge. The financial support from one person may be small, but it adds up when millions of people give a few dollars.

The reader should also write letters to the members of the House of Representatives and the Senate, especially the politicians who represent the reader's congressional district and state. The reader should request that his or her elected officials initiate and support the investigation of any federal judge who makes constitutional law, for consideration of impeachment and removal from office. The stated reason should be that such a federal judge is taking democracy away from the American people. Such a letter should be written each time the reader becomes aware of a federal court decision which the reader believes is law-making, rather than the application of actual constitutional principles set forth in the U.S. Constitution. The specific case should be identified or described. A sample letter is provided in Appendix B.

The reader may believe that his or her Representative or Senator would not support such an effort. However, that should not stop such requests. The elected official is much less likely to actively oppose an effort to impeach and remove a federal judge, if a substantial portion of the elected official's constituency supports an effort to do so. The main way such a member of the House or the Senate will know that many people in his or her district or state oppose judicial law-making is by receiving direct communications from those people.

The reader should also financially support those political organizations which seek to remove appropriate judges from office, and those which fight politicians who oppose removal of law-making judges from office. It takes funds to do these things. Even if the amount the reader can give is small, it adds up and is an indication of "grass roots" support. That is very important for people who are conducting such activities to know. They may be able to obtain funding from other sources due to the extent of interest expressed by voters.

The reader should also express his or her views in public and private forums, such as periodicals, schools, civic and religious organizations, workplaces, etc. That is what successful political movements in America have always done.

Our constitutional rights, and our right to self-government, are at stake. For our children and grandchildren, those freedoms are subject to even greater threats if judicial rule spreads. Judicial rule will grow unless we fight to stop it.

I do not want my generation to be the one that sat by and let federal judges develop legal doctrines which were the basis for taking away the freedoms Americans enjoy, including the right to vote on important issues. Many people in this and earlier generations have died to protect America's freedoms. We should at least fight vigorously in the political arena to keep them.

How Judges Should Be Considered For Removal From Office

The reader should understand that a thorough evaluation should be done before a federal judge is targeted for impeachment and removal. I have consciously avoided mentioning the name of any current law-making federal judge in this book. The subject of which current federal judge are appropriate candidates for removal is beyond the scope of this book.

Although I do not doubt that the present federal courts, including the present U.S. Supreme Court, have exceeded their power by illegally making constitutional law, I have personally not conducted an investigation for any current federal judges. That should be done before a particular judge is targeted for removal.

A current federal judge should not be held responsible for the actions of federal judges that no longer occupy any judicial office because they have retired or died. Federal judges are, for the most part, supposed to apply the law that higher courts have established, even if that law is improper. Federal judges who only follow the precedents of higher courts should not be considered for impeachment and removal from office. On the other hand, a judge's claim that he or she is following precedent may not be accurate.

Nor, in my view, should a judge normally be removed from office for refusing to cut back on illegal constitutional principles that were established by other judges in earlier cases, within the same court. However, if a current federal judge tries to expand an illegal constitutional doctrine such as the "separation of church and state" doctrine, that judge appropriately risks impeachment and removal from office. That is true even if the attempted expansion of an unconstitutional doctrine is small. Dramatic changes to the Constitution have occurred through a sequence of small changes in a number of cases.

When a judge has illegally seized political power, removal is proper to consider. Legislators and executive politicians are regularly removed from office through elections. Therefore, it is appropriate for a federal judge, who injects himself or herself into the political realm of lawmaking, to receive serious consideration for impeachment or removal from office.

Any Desirable Unconstitutional Principles That Are Eliminated Should Be Considered For Legislative Action

If we, as Americans, are successful in motivating federal judges to eliminate unconstitutional legal principles such as the "separation of church and state" doctrine, we should consider motivating our legislators to enact into law "desirable" principles that have been eliminated from constitutional law. For example, I believe that *mandatory* prayer or Bible study for religious purposes in government institutions should be prohibited by law. Of course, "desirable" laws should be created only if enacted by a democratic process.

The reader should be reminded, however, that impeachment and removal does not change constitutional law. That can only be done by the U.S. Supreme Court after removal, or by a democratically-ratified constitutional amendment.

Some people claim that they fear a "theocracy" in America, and that the "separation of church and state" doctrine protects against "theocracy." They proceed to argue that the "separation of church and state" doctrine should be retained and expanded in our constitutional law, because of its protection against "theocracy."

This view is irrational fear-mongering. If a "theocracy" in America was a realistic possibility, America would have had one in the eighteenth and nineteenth centuries. When America was founded, the vast majority of Americans were active Christians. In spite of these circumstances, there was no "theocracy" in America. Adherents to "non-believism" and other faiths have thrived quite well in America, due to constitutional rights and protections that are guaranteed to all Americans. This has been true in spite of the absence of any "separation of church and state" doctrine during the eighteenth, the nineteenth, and the first half of the twentieth centuries. In fact, there was *no federal limitation* on the religious practices of state governments during that entire time period.

I would also like to specifically address those Americans who adhere to a religious faith holding that the New Testament portion of the Bible is scripture. I am one of those Americans.

In the New Testament, Jesus Christ never tried to force people to adhere to his teachings. He tried only to *persuade* people to believe in Him. He consistently said that "His kingdom" was not of this world. Therefore, I believe that Americans who are part of such a faith should not attempt to have laws passed, or to engage in government-initiated practices, that would, for example, require people to pray in the name of Jesus Christ, or to read the Bible for religious purposes. People's hearts cannot be changed by force of law, or by forced observance.

I am not, however, saying that it is appropriate to suppress the voluntary expression of religious beliefs, including attempts to persuade others to believe. Nor is it appropriate to suppress the passive posting of historical items in governmental institutions or symbols because of their religious content.

People's Views Regarding God Necessarily Affect Their Political Views

I am also not saying that the beliefs of people who adhere to a biblical religious faith, or another religious faith, should not influence how those people vote on abortion, same-sex marriage, or other political issues. All laws reflect a moral judgment of one kind or another. People who deny that are either not truthful, or have a very narrow, inappropriate definition of the word "moral." People's beliefs or non-beliefs about the nature of the universe inevitably affect people's opinions about what the law should be, and thus their voting patterns.

Most people who, for example, believe there is no god, or that beliefs about god are irrelevant to man's laws, would likely find no problem with the government encouraging homosexuality or abortion. Most people who adhere to such a belief system would likely conclude that we actually, or effectively, live in a materialistic universe with no overarching moral imperatives. Therefore, we, as completely independent agents in the universe, can make our laws whatever we wish them to be. The only moral legitimacy is that which either the individual or the government determines. The appropriate laws in our society are those that are *chosen by individuals or the government*, with no higher moral value. To most people who adhere to such beliefs, abortion and homosexuality would likely have no lower or higher moral position than any other choice. In other words, to such persons, it is *solely* a matter of what human beings *choose*, either individually or collectively, that governs what the law should be.

It is possible that a person who believes that god is of no relevance would be against laws encouraging abortion or homosexuality, if that person had an additional belief that opposed the moral consequences of such activities, or had sociological or physical reasons for opposing such laws. However, the absence of a moral imperative concerning abortion or homosexuality resulting from such a person's view of the nature of the universe, would tend to influence such a person to support laws encouraging abortion or homosexuality.

On the other hand, a person who believes in a god is much more likely to be opposed to laws encouraging abortion or homosexuality, because of that person's views of the nature of the universe. Various moral imperatives almost always follow from such a theistic faith. For example, most theistic religions have commands against homosexuality as an immoral act in their scriptures. In both the Old and New Testaments of the Bible, for instance, homosexuality is grouped together with adultery as an immoral act. Furthermore, marriage between a man and a woman is a God-ordained institution in the Old and New Testaments. These, as well as sociological considerations, are likely to affect such a person's opinions about laws encouraging homosexuality.

Some people who profess belief in a god may ignore or attempt to explain away scriptural commands against homo-sexuality. However, those people are a small portion of those who believe in a god who cares about human affairs.

For a person who adheres to a theistic faith, the outcome on the abortion issue would normally turn on whether the person believes that a fetus is a human being. If so, abortion is murder. All theistic faiths I am aware of hold murder to be immoral. The moral interest of another person such as the woman carrying the fetus (apart from a threat to the woman's life), does not outweigh the moral interest of the fetus, as a human being, to live. For those who believe that a fetus is not a human being, but instead is another form of life that does not warrant protection, termination of the fetus's existence would normally be acceptable (although perhaps not preferred) by even a person of a theistic faith.

It is my opinion that the scientific evidence, as well as Biblical scriptural passages, establish that a fetus *is* a human being. It is, therefore, my view that abortion is murder and should be illegal.

It is also my view that abortion is not a legitimate constitutional right. That "right" was illegally created by the U.S. Supreme Court. Even some legal experts who support abortion agree that abortion is not a legitimate constitutional right.

In conclusion, the beliefs of a person about the existence or relevance of a god, are very likely to affect the views of that person on what the law should be. Those who insist that religious people not allow their religious beliefs to affect their political opinions, or their voting patterns, are inappropriately advocating a form of censorship of thought. They are also, in my view, being hypocritical because their views of the moral or amoral nature of the universe affect their own views on what laws our nation should be.

Political And Religious Discourse And History Should Be Free And Open In Both Public And Private Institutions

The adherents to one form or another of "non-believism," as well as other belief systems, are invited to enter into a free and open discourse with adherents of theistic faiths on the legal and political issues that face our nation. We should engage in such a discourse in both public and private institutions with mutual respect for each other and each other's views. We can do that even though we disagree. There should be no censorship of religious or secular views in public institutions. Nor should there be any suppression of the history of our nation, or the history of the world in general, whether or not the history is religious.

When there is controversy about these issues, the appropriate course of action should be decided by a democratic process, or by democratically agreed-upon constitutional laws. Federal judges should not be permitted to impose their views of what constitutional law should be on the American people. Federal judges' votes should count no more, and no less, than those of other Americans. Judges should try to impose their personal views only in political forums and the ballot box, not in judicial opinions.

Those Americans who insist on imposing their views on other Americans through the courts, without any democratic process, have a war on their hands. Although that war is about cultural values, it is nevertheless a political war. I believe I am expressing the views of most Americans when I say that Americans do not intend to stand by and let a few judges impose their beliefs on them or their children. Americans insist on the right to vote on the relevant issues. Those who wish to deny the right of Americans to vote on these important political issues should be excluded from judicial office, because what they are doing is unconstitutional and denies the American people their right to self-government.

APPENDIX A

The Constitution of The United States of America

We the people of the United States, in Order to form a more perfect Union, establish Justice, insure domestic Tranquility, provide for the common defence, promote the general Welfare, and secure the Blessings of Liberty to ourselves and our Posterity, do ordain and establish this Constitution for the United States of America.

. . .

ARTICLE I
SECTION 1. All legislative Powers herein granted shall be vested in a Congress of the United States which shall consist of a Senate and House of Representatives.

SECTION 2. The House of Representatives shall be composed of Members chosen every second Year by the People of the several States, . . .

. . .

The House of Representatives shall chuse their Speaker and other Officers; and shall have the sole Power of Impeachment.

SECTION 3. The Senate of United States shall be composed of two Senators from each State, chosen by the

Legislature thereof, for six Years; and each Senator shall have one Vote.

. . .

The Senate shall have the sole Power to try all Impeachments. When sitting for that Purpose, they shall be on Oath or Affirmative. When the President of the United States is tried, the Chief Justice shall preside: And no Person shall be convicted without the Concurrence of two thirds of the Members present.

Judgment in Cases of Impeachment shall not extend further than to removal from Office, and disqualification to hold and enjoy any Office of honor, Trust or Profit under the United States: but the Party convicted shall nevertheless be liable and subject to Indictment, Trial, Judgment and Punishment, according to Law.

. . .

SECTION 7.

. . .

Every Bill which shall have passed the House of Representatives and the Senate, shall, before it becomes a Law, be presented to the President of the United Sates; If he approve he shall sign it, but if not he shall return it, with his Objections to that House in which it shall have originated, who shall enter the Objections at large on their Journal, and proceed to reconsider it. If after such Reconsideration two thirds of that House shall agree to pass the Bill, it shall be sent, together with the Objections, to the other House, by which it shall likewise be reconsidered, and if approved by two thirds of that House, it shall become a Law.

. . .

Every Order, Resolution, or Vote to which the Concurrence of the Senate and House of Representatives may be necessary (except on a question of Adjournment) shall be presented to the President of the United States; and before the Same shall take Effect, shall be approved by him, or being disapproved by him, shall be repassed by two thirds of the Senate and House of Representatives, according to the Rules and Limitations prescribed in the Case of a Bill.

SECTION 8. The Congress shall have Power To lay and collect Taxes, Duties, Imposts and Excises, to pay the Debts and provide for the common Defence and general Welfare of the United State; but all Duties, Imposts and Excises shall be uniform throughout the United States;

To borrow money on the credit of the United States;

To regulate Commerce with foreign Nations, and among the several States, and with the Indian Tribes;

To establish an uniform Rule of Naturalization, and uniform Laws on the subject of Bankruptcies throughout the United States;

To coin Money, regulate the Value thereof, and of foreign Coin, and fix the Standard of Weights and Measures;

To provide for the Punishment of counterfeiting the Securities and current Coin of the United States;

To establish Post Offices and post Road;

To promote the Progress of Science and useful Arts, by securing for limited Times to Authors and Inventors the exclusive Right to their respective Writings and Discoveries;

To constitute Tribunals inferior to the supreme Court;

To define and punish Piracies and Felonies committed on the high Seas, and Offenses against the Law of Nations;

To declare War, grant Letters of Marque and Reprisal, and make Rules concerning Captures on Land and Water;

To raise and support Armies, but no Appropriation of Money to that Use shall be for a longer Term than two Years;

To provide and maintain a Navy;

To make Rules for the Government and Regulation of the land and naval Forces;

To provide for calling forth the Militia to execute the Laws of the Union, suppress Insurrections and repel Invasions;

To provide for organizing, arming, and disciplining the Militia, and for governing such Part of them as may be employed in the Service of the United States, reserving to the States respectively, the Appointment of the Officers, and the Authority of training the Militia according to the discipline prescribed by Congress;

To exercise exclusive Legislation in all Cases whatsoever, over such District (not exceeding ten Miles square) as may, by Cession of particular States, and the acceptance of Congress, become the Seat of the Government of the United States, and to exercise like Authority over all Places purchased by the Consent of the Legislature of the State in which the Same shall be, for the Erection of Forts, Magazines, Arsenals, dock-Yards, and other needful Buildings; -And

To make all Laws which shall be necessary and proper for carrying into Execution the foregoing Powers, and all other Powers vested by this Constitution in the Government of the United States, or in any Department or Officer thereof.

. . .

ARTICLE II

SECTION 1. The executive Power shall be vested in a President of the United States of America. He shall hold his Office during the Term of four Years, and together with the Vice-President, chosen for the same term, be elected as follows:

Each State shall appoint, in such Manner as the Legislature thereof may direct, a Number of Electors, equal to the whole Number of Senators and Representatives to which the State may be entitled in the Congress: but no Senator or Representative, or Person holding an Office of

Trust or Profit under the United States, shall be appointed an Elector.

[The Electors shall meet in their respective States, and vote by Ballot for two persons, of whom one at least shall not be an Inhabitant of the same State with themselves. And they shall make a List of all the Persons voted for, and of the Number of Votes for each; which List they shall sign and certify, and transmit sealed to the Seat of the Government of the United States, directed to the President of the Senate. The President of the Senate shall, in the Presence of the Senate and House of Representative, open all the Certificates, and the Votes shall then be counted. The Person having the greatest Number of Votes shall be the President, if such Number be a Majority of the whole Number of Electors appointed; and if there be more than one who have such Majority, and have an equal Number of Votes, then the House of Representatives shall immediately chuse by Ballot one of them for President; and if no Person have a Majority, then from the five highest on the List the said House shall in like Manner chuse the President. But in chusing the President, the Votes shall be taken by States, the Representation from each State having one Vote; A quorum for this Purpose shall consist of a Member or Members from two-thirds of the States, and a Majority of all the States shall be necessary to a Choice. In every Case, after the Choice of the President, the Person having the greatest Number of Votes of the Electors shall be the Vice President. But if there should remain two or more who have equal Votes, the Senate shall chuse from them by Ballot the Vice-President.]

The Congress may determine the Time of chusing the Electors, and the Day on which they shall give their Votes; which Day shall be the same throughout the United States.

. . .

SECTION 2.

. . .

. . . he [the President] shall nominate, and by and with the Advice and Consent of the Senate, shall appoint Ambassadors, other public Ministers and Consuls, Judges of the supreme Court, and all other Officers of the United States, whose Appointments are not herein otherwise provided for, and which shall be established by Law:

. . .

SECTION 4. The President, Vice President and all civil Officers of the United States, shall be removed from Office on Impeachment for, and Conviction of, Treason, Bribery, or other high Crimes and Misdemeanors.

ARTICLE III

SECTION 1. The judicial Power of the United States, shall be vested in one supreme Court, and in such inferior Courts as the Congress may from time to time ordain and establish. The Judges, both of the supreme and inferior Courts, shall hold their Offices during good Behaviour, and shall, at stated Times, receive for their Services a Compensation which shall not be diminished during their Continuance in Office.

SECTION 2. The judicial Power shall extend to all Cases, in Law and Equity, arising under this Constitution, the Laws of the United States, and Treaties made, or which shall be made, under their Authority; -to all Cases affecting Ambassadors, other public Ministers and Consuls; -to all Cases of admiralty and maritime Jurisdiction; -to Controversies to which the United States shall be a Party; -to Controversies between two or more States; -between a State and Citizens of another State; -between Citizens of different States; -between Citizens of the same State claiming Lands under Grants of different States, and between a State, or the Citizens thereof, and foreign States, Citizens or Subjects.

. . .

ARTICLE V

The Congress, whenever two-thirds of both Houses shall deem it necessary, shall propose Amendments to this Constitution, or, on the Application of the Legislatures of two-thirds of the several States, shall call a Convention for proposing Amendments, which, in either Case, shall be valid to all Intents and Purposes, as part of this Constitution, when ratified by the Legislatures of three-fourths of the several States, or by Conventions in three-fourths thereof, as the one or the other Mode of Ratification may be proposed by the Congress;

. . .

. . .no State, without its Consent, shall be deprived of its equal Suffrage in the Senate.

ARTICLE VI

. . .

This Constitution, and the Laws of the United States which shall be made in Pursuance thereof; and all Treaties made, or which shall be made, under the Authority of the United States, shall be the supreme Law of the Land; and the Judges in every State shall be bound thereby, any Thing in the Constitution or Laws of any State to the Contrary notwithstanding.

. . .

The Senators and Representatives before mentioned, and the Members of the several State Legislatures, and all executive and judicial Officers, both of the United States and of the several States, shall be bound by Oath or Affirmation, to support this Constitution;

. . .

BILL OF RIGHTS

ARTICLE I. [First Amendment]
Congress shall make no law respecting an establishment of religion, or prohibiting the free exercise thereof; or abridging the freedom of speech, or of the press; or the right of the people peaceably to assemble, and to petition the Government for a redress of grievances.

. . .

ARTICLE V. [Fifth Amendment]
No person shall . . . be deprived of life, liberty, or property, without due process of law. . .

. . .

ARTICLE VII. [Seventh Amendment]
In suits at common law, where the value in controversy shall exceed twenty dollars, the right of trial by jury shall be preserved, and no fact tried by a jury, shall be otherwise re-examined in any Court of the United States, than according to the rules of the common law.

ARTICLE VIII. [Eighth Amendment]
Excessive bail shall not be required, nor excessive fines imposed, nor cruel and unusual punishment inflicted.

. . .

ARTICLE X. [Tenth Amendment]
The powers not delegated to the United States by the Constitution, nor prohibited by it to the States, are reserved to the States respectively, or to the people.

. . .

OTHER CONSTITUTIONAL AMENDMENTS

ARTICLE XIV. [Fourteenth Amendment]
SECTION 1.　　. . . No State shall make or enforce any law which shall abridge the privileges or immunities of

citizens of the United States; nor shall any State deprive any person of life, liberty, or property, without due process of law; nor deny to any person within its jurisdiction the equal protection of the laws.

APPENDIX B

Dear [Senator…][Representative…]:

I am writing about my strong opposition to a judicial decision of [name of the federal court in which the decision was made]. The court decision was [name the decision by the names of the parties (e.g., <u>Everson v. Ewing Township Board of Education</u>)][or describe the decision (e.g., the decision to incorporate the "separation of church and state" doctrine into the First Amendment)].

I believe that you should seriously consider seeking the impeachment and removal of the judge[s] responsible for the foregoing decision from judicial office. The basis for impeachment and removal is that this [these] judge[s] has [have] abused judicial power by making constitutional law in violation of the separation of powers doctrine in the U.S. Constitution. Such seizures of governmental power take the right of self-government away from the American people.

Sincerely Yours,

[Name and address*]

*The address is necessary so that the politician can verify you are in his/her district of representation and are a registered voter

ENDNOTES

Chapter 1

1. <u>Everson v. Board of Education of Ewing Township</u>, 330 U.S. 1 (19747).
2. <u>Brandon v. Board of Education of Guilderland Central School District</u>, 635 F.2d 971, 975 (2nd Cir. 1980).
3. <u>Lawrence v. Texas</u>, 539 U.S. 558 (2003).
4. <u>Lawrence</u>, 539 U.S. at 605 (dissenting opinion by J. Scalia, Rehnquist and Thomas).
5. Robertson, Pat, <u>Courting Disaster</u> (Nashville, Integrity Publishers, 2004), at 191-92.
6. <u>Newdow v. U.S. Congress</u>, 292 F.3d 597 (2002).
7. <u>Elk Grove Unified School District v. Newdow</u>, 124 S.Ct. 2301 (2004).
8. Mayer, David N., <u>The Constitutional Thought of Thomas Jefferson</u> (Charlottesville, University Press of Virginia, 1994), at 280.
9. Rossiter, Clinton, <u>The Federalist Papers</u>, "No. 81: Hamilton" (New York, Penguin Group, 1961), at 485.
10. Rossiter (n. 9, <u>supra</u>), "Introduction," at vii.

Chapter 2

1. Mayer, David N., <u>The Constitutional Thought of</u>

Thomas Jefferson (Charlottesville, University Press of Virginia, 1994), at 280.

2. Bork, Robert H., <u>Coercing Virtue: The Worldwide Rule of Judges</u> (Washington D.C., The AEI Press, 2003), at 5-6.
3. Bork (n. 2, <u>supra</u>), at 11-12.
4. Mayer (n. 1, <u>supra</u>), at 287.
5. U.S. Constitution, Article I (see Appendix A).
6. U.S. Constitution, Article II (see Appendix A).
7. U.S. Constitution, Article III (see Appendix A).
8. U.S. Constitution, Article III, Section 1 (see Appendix A).
9. Mayer (n. 1, <u>supra</u>), at 280.
10. U.S. Constitution, Article III, Section 2 (see Appendix A).
11. Rossiter, Clinton, <u>The Federalist Papers</u>, "No. 81: Hamilton" (New York, Penguin Group, 1961), at 485.
12. Mayer (n. 1, <u>supra</u>), at 280.
13. Mayer (n. 1, <u>supra</u>), at 287.

Chapter 3

1. Mayer, David N., <u>The Constitutional Thought of Thomas Jefferson</u> (Charlottesville, University Press of Virginia, 1994), at xi (emphasis added).
2. Rakove, Jack N., <u>James Madison: Writings</u> (New York, Literary Classics, 1999), at 508 (emphasis added).
3. <u>Bowsher v. Synar</u>, 478 U.S. 714, 721-22 (1986) (emphasis added).
4. U.S. Constitution, Article I, Section 1 (see Appendix A)(emphasis added).
5. U.S. Constitution Article I, Section 8, last paragraph (see Appendix A)(emphasis added).
6. First Amendment to U.S. Constitution (See Appendix A)(emphasis added).

7. U.S. Constitution, Article I, Section 3 (see Appendix A).
8. U.S. Constitution, Article I, Section 2 (see Appendix A).
9. U.S. Constitution, Article II, Section 1 (see Appendix A) (emphasis added).
10. <u>Marbury v. Madison</u>, 1 Cranch 137 (1803).

Chapter 4

1. U.S. Constitution, Article III, Section 1 (see Appendix A) (emphasis added).
2. U.S. Constitution, Article III, Section 2 (see Appendix A) (emphasis added).
3. U.S. Constitution, Article II, Section 2, paragraph 2 (see Appendix A) (emphasis added).
4. U.S. Constitution, Article III, Section 1 (see Appendix A).
5. Rossiter, Clinton, <u>The Federalist Papers</u>, "No. 81: Hamilton" (New York, Penguin Group, 1961), at 484-85 (emphasis added).
6. Mayer, David N., <u>The Constitutional Thought of Thomas Jefferson</u> (Charlottesville, University Press of Virginia, 1994), at 270 (emphasis added).
7. <u>Marbury v. Madision</u>, 1 Cranch 137 (1803).
8. Kramer, Larry D., <u>The People Themselves: Popular Constitutionalism and Judicial Review</u> (New York, Oxford University Press, 2004), at 183.
9. Rossiter, (n. 5, <u>supra</u>), at 484-85.
10. Rossiter, (n. 5, <u>supra</u>) at 484-85.
11. U.S. Constitution, Article III, Section 2 (see Appendix A).

Chapter 5

1. U.S. Constitution, Article I, Section 8 (see Appendix A).

2. Tenth Amendment to U.S. Constitution (see Appendix A).
3. Mayer, David N., <u>The Constitutional Thought of Thomas Jefferson</u>, (Charlottesville, University Press of Virginia, 1994), at 288.
4. Tenth Amendment to U.S. Constitution (Appendix A).
5. Mayer (n. 3, <u>supra</u>), at 277 (emphasis added).
6. Mayer (n. 3, <u>supra</u>), at 287.
7. Mayer (n. 3, <u>supra</u>), at 287 ("all know the influence of interest on the mind of man, and how consciously his judgment is warped by that influence") and at 292-93.
8. Mayer (n. 3, <u>supra</u>) , at 287.
9. U.S. Constitution, Article VI, Clause 2 (see Appendix A)(emphasis added).
10. U.S. Constitution, Article V (see Appendix A).
11. U.S. Constitution, Article V (see Appendix A)(emphasis added).

Chapter 6

1. First Amendment to U.S. Constitution (see Appendix A).
2. <u>Everson v. Board of Education of Ewing Township</u>, 330 U.S. 1 (1947).
3. <u>Brandon v. Board of Education of Guilderland Central School District</u>, 635 F.2d 971, 975 (2nd Cir. 1980).
4. <u>Brandon</u> (n. 3, <u>supra</u>), at 975.
5. Staver, Matthew D., <u>Faith and Freedom</u> (Wheaton, Crossway Books, 1995), Forward by Charles E. Rice, at xii; see also <u>Elk Grove Unified School District v. Newdow</u>, 124 s. ct. 2301, 2330 (2004) (Thomas, J., dissenting).
6. <u>Zelman v. Simmons Harris</u>, 536 U.S. 639, 720

(2002) (dissenting opinion by J. Stevens, Souter and Breyer).

7. Fourteenth Amendment to the U.S. Constitution (see Appendix A).
8. Cantwell v. Connecticut, 310 U.S. 296 (1940).
9. Everson (n.2, supra), 330 U.S. 1.
10. Fifth Amendment to U.S. Constitution (see Appendix A).
11. Staver (n.5, supra), at 25.
12. Staver (n.5, supra), at 25.
13. Staver (n.5, supra), at 25.
14. Staver (n.5, supra), at 26 n.10.
15. Bowsher v. Synar, 478 U.S. 714, 727 (1986) (emphasis added).

Chapter 7

1. Everson v. Board of Education of Ewing Township, 330 U.S. 1 (1947).
2. Everson, 330 U.S. at 18 (emphasis added).
3. Mayer, David N., The Constitutional Thought of Thomas Jefferson (Charlottesville, University Press of Virginia, 1994), at 287.
4. Everson, 330 U.S. at 16 (emphasis added).
5. Everson, 330 U.S. at 18 (emphasis added).
6. Everson, 330 U.S. at 60-61.
7. Engel v. Vitale, 370 U.S. 421 (1962).
8. School District of Arlington Township v. Schempp, 374 U.S. 203 (1963).
9. Zelman v. Simmons Harris, 536 U.S. 639, 720 (2000) (dissenting opinion).
10. Mayer (n.3, supra), at 287.
11. www.lonang.com/exlibris/misc/danbury.htm
12. Mayer (n.3, supra), at 287.
13. Staver, Matthew D., Faith and Freedom (Wheaton, Crossway Books, 1995), at 30.

14. Staver (n.13, <u>supra</u>), at 30.
15. <u>Wallace v. Jaffree</u>, 472 U.S. 38, 92 (1985)(Rehnquist, J., dissenting).
16. <u>Wallace</u> (n. 15, <u>supra</u>), at 92.
17. <u>Wallace</u> (n. 15, <u>supra</u>), at 94 (citing 1 Annals of Congress 434).
18. <u>Wallace</u> (n. 15, <u>supra</u>), at 96 (citing 1 Annals of Congress 731).
19. <u>Wallace</u> (n. 15, <u>supra</u>), at 96-97 (citing 1 Annals of Congress 731).
20. <u>Wallace</u> (n. 15, <u>supra</u>), at 95 (citing 1 Annals of Congress 729).
21. <u>Wallace</u> (n. 15, <u>supra</u>), at 97 (citing 1 Annals of Congress 766).
22. <u>Wallace</u> (n. 15, <u>supra</u>), at 96 (citing 1 Annals of Congress 730-31).
23. <u>Wallace</u> (n. 15, <u>supra</u>), at 97 (citing Antieau, A. Downey, & E. Roberts, <u>Freedom from Federal Establishment</u>, at 130 (1964)).
24. <u>Wallace</u> (n. 15, <u>supra</u>), at 97.
25. <u>Wallace</u> (n. 15, <u>supra</u>), at 96 (citing 1 Annals of Congress 731).
26. <u>Allegheny County v. ACLU</u>, 492 U.S. 573, 590 (1989).
27. <u>Wallace v. Jaffree</u>, 472 U.S. 38, 52-53 (1985).
28. Staver (n. 13, <u>supra</u>, at 19-20) (emphasis added) (citing Paul Blanshard, "Three Cheers for Our Secular State," <u>The Humanist</u>, March/April 1976, p. 17).
29. Staver (n. 13, <u>supra</u>), Foreward by Charles E. Rice, at xiv (citing Bozarth, "On Keeping God Alive," <u>American Atheist</u>, 1977, 7-8) (emphasis added).
30. <u>Lemon v. Kurzman</u>, 403 U.S. 602 (1971).
31. <u>Allegheny County</u> (n. 26, <u>supra</u>), at 595-96.
32. <u>Citizens Against Rent Control Coalition of Fair</u>

housing v. City of Berkeley, 454 U.S. 290, 295 (1981) (emphasis added).

Chapter 8

1. Brandon v. Board of Education of Guilderland Central School District, 635 F. 2d 971 (2nd Cir 1980), cert. denied, 454 U.S. 1123 (1981).
2. Brandon, 635 F. 2d at 977.
3. Brandon, 635 F. 2d at 977.
4. Chess v. Widmar, 635 F.2d 1310, 1316 (6th Cir. 1980).
5. Brandon, 635 F.2d at 978 (emphasis added).
6. Brandon, 635 F.2d at 978-979.
7. Brandon, 635 F.2d at 973 (emphasis added).
8. Brandon, 635 F.2d at 978 (emphasis added).
9. Brandon, 635 F.2d at 975 (emphasis added).
10. Lubbock Civil Liberties Union v. Lubbock Independent School District, 669 F.2d 1038 (5th Cir. 1982).
11. Lubbock, 669 F.2d at 1041 (emphasis added).
12. Lubbock, 669 F.2d at 1045 (emphasis added).
13. Lubbock, 669 F.2d at 1046 (emphasis added).
14. Bender v. Williamsport Area School District, 741 F.2d 538 (3rd Cir. 1984).
15. Bender, 741 F.2d at 550-57.
16. Zelman v. Simmons Harris, 536 U.S. 639, 720 (2002) (dissenting opinion).
17. Bender, 741 F.2d at 554 n. 22 (emphasis added).
18. Allegheny County v. ACLU, 492 U.S. 573, 590 (1989).
19. Donovan v. Punxsutawney Area School Board, 336 F.3d 211 (2003); Pope v. East Brunswick School Board of Education, 12 F.3d 1244 (1993).
20. Board of Education of the Westside Community Schools v. Mergens, 496 U.S. 226 (1990).

21. <u>Mergens</u>, 496 U.S. at 248.
22. <u>Mergens</u>, 496 U.S. at 250-52.
23. <u>Mergens</u>, 496 U.S. at 253.
24. <u>Lee v. Weisman</u>, 505 U.S. 577 (1992).
25. <u>Mergens</u>, 496 U.S. at 260-61.
26. <u>Mergens</u>, 496 U.S. at 269-70.

Chapter 9

1. <u>Stone v. Graham</u>, 449 U.S. 39 (1980).
2. <u>Stone</u>, at 39 n. 1.
3. <u>Stone</u>, at 41.
4. <u>Stone</u>, at 42.
5. <u>Lynch v. Donnelly</u>, 465 U.S. 668, 677 (1984).
6. <u>Corpus Juris Secundum</u> (St. Paul, West, 2002), vol. 15A, "Common Law," §§ 1,7, and 8, at pp. 24 and 29.
7. <u>Stone</u>, at 42.
8. <u>Wallace v. Jaffree</u>, 472 U.S. 38, 52-53 (1985).
9. <u>Allegheny County v. ACLU</u>, 492 U.S. 573, 590(1989).
10. <u>Encarta World English Dictionary</u>, (St. Martin's Press, New York, 1999), at 1620.
11. <u>Glassroth v. Moore</u>, 335 F.3d 1282 (11th Cir. 2003); <u>McGinely v. Houston</u>, 361 F.3d 1328 (11th Cir. 2004).
12. <u>Glassroth</u>, 335 F.3d at 1294-95 (emphasis added).
13. <u>McGinely</u>, 361 F.3d at 1332-33.
14. <u>Allegheny County</u>, 492 U.S. at 590.
15. <u>McGinely</u>, 361 F.3d at 1332.
16. See <u>Committee for Public Education and Religious Liberty v. Regan</u>, 444 U.S. 646, 671 (1980)(J. Stevens); <u>Wallace</u>, 472 U.S. at 110 (1985)(C.J. Rehnquist); <u>Bishop of the Church of Jesus Christ of Latter-Day Saints v. Amons</u>, 483 U.S. 327, 346 (1987)(J.O'Connor); <u>Allegheny County</u>, 492 U.S. at

655-56 (J. Kennedy); <u>Lee v. Weisman</u>, 505 U.S. 577, 644 (1992)(J. Scalia and J. Thomas).

17. <u>Wallace</u>, 472 U.S. at 110.

18. <u>Wallace</u>, 472 U.S. at 61.

19. <u>Bowsher v. Synar</u>, 478 U.S. 714, 727 (1986).

20. Mayer, David N., <u>The Constitutional Thought of Thomas Jefferson</u> (Charlottesville, University Press of Virginia, 1994), at 280.

21. Rossiter, Clinton, <u>The Federalist Papers</u> (New York, Penguin Books, 1961), "No. 51: Madison," at 322.

22. Rossiter, Clinton, <u>The Federalist Papers</u>, "No. 81, Hamilton," (New York, Penguin Group, 1961), at 485.

23. <u>Van Orden v. Perry</u>, 351 F.3d 173 (5th Cir. 2003).

24. <u>ACLU of Kentucky v. McCreary County</u>, 354 F.3d 438 (6th Cir. 2003).

25. <u>Van Orden</u>, 351 F.3d at 176.

26. <u>McCreary County</u>, 354 F.3d at 443.

27. <u>McCreary County</u>, at 444.

28. <u>McCreary County</u>, at 448.

29. <u>McCreary County</u>, at 461.

30. <u>ACLU of Ohio Foundation, Inc. v. Ashbrook</u>, 375 F. 3d 484 (6th Cir. 2004); <u>Adland v. Russ</u>, 307 F. 3d 471 (6th Cir. 2002), <u>cert. denied</u>, 538 U.S. 999 (2003); <u>Books v. City of Elkhart</u>, 235 F.3d 471 (7th Cir. 2000), <u>cert. denied</u>, 532 U.S. 1058 (2001).

31. <u>Indiana Civil Liberties Union v. O'Bannon</u>, 259 F.3d 766 (7th Cir. 2001), <u>cert. denied</u>, 534 U.S. 1162 (2002).

32. <u>ACLU of Nebraska Foundation v. City of Plattsmouth</u>, 358 F. 3d 1020 (8th Cir. 2004).

33. <u>Van Orden</u>, 351 F.3d at 175-76.

34. <u>See</u> <u>Modrovich v. Allegheny County</u>, 385 F. 3d 397 (3rd Cir. 2004)(a Ten Commandments plaque was mounted on a wall in the courtyard of a county

courthouse since 1918); <u>King v. Richmond County</u>, 331 F.3d 1271 (11th Cir. 2003)(a state court seal had two tablets representing the Ten Commandments for a period of 130 years); <u>Freethought Society of Greater Philadelphia v. Chester County</u>, 334 F.3d 247 (3d Cir. 2003)(a Ten Commandments plaque was mounted near the entrance of a county courthouse since 1920).

Chapter 10

1. Mayer, David N., <u>The Constitutional Thought Of Thomas Jefferson</u> (Charlottesville, University Press of Virginia, 1994), at 292-93.
2. Mayer (n. 1, <u>supra</u>), at 287.
3. Rossiter, Clinton, <u>The Federalist Papers</u>, "No. 51: Madison" (New York, Penguin Books, 1961), at 322.
4. <u>Bowsher v. Synar</u>, 478 U.S. 714, 727 (1986).
5. <u>Trop v. Dalles</u>, 356 U.S. 100-101 (1958) (emphasis added).
6. Robertson, Pat, <u>Courting Disaster</u> (Nashville, Integrity Publishers, 2004), at 84 (citing William J. Brennan Jr., "What the Constitution Requires," <u>New York Times</u>, April 28, 1996).
7. Tribe, Lawrence H., <u>God Save This Honorable Court</u> (New York, Random House, 1985), at 46 (emphasis added except as to "always").
8. Tribe (n. 7, <u>supra</u>), at 47 (emphasis added).
9. Tribe (n. 7, <u>supra</u>), at 48.
10. Tribe, <u>supra</u>, at 48 (emphasis added).
11. <u>Bowsher</u>, 478 U.S. at 727.
12. <u>www.uscourts.gov/newsroom/2004YearEnd Report.pdf</u>, "2004 Year-End Report on the Federal Judiciary," at 5.
13. "2004 Year-End Report" (n. 12, <u>supra</u>), at 6.

14. Levy, L.W., Karst, K.L. and Mahoney, D.J., <u>Encyclopedia of the American Constitution</u> (New York, MacMillan, 1986), "Impeachment," by Raoul Berger, at 960.
15. Rossiter (n. 3 <u>supra</u>), "No. 79: Hamilton," at 474 (emphasis added).

Chapter 11

1. U.S. Constitution, Article III, Section 1 (See Appendix A).
2. U.S. Constitution, Article VI, Clause 3 (See Appendix A).
3. U.S. Constitution, Article I, Section 2, Clause 5 (emphasis added)(see Appendix A)
4. U.S. Constitution, Article I, Section 3, Clause 6 (emphasis added)(see Appendix A).
5. U.S. Constitution, Article I, Section 3, Clause 6 (emphasis added)(see Appendix A)
6. U.S. Constitution, Article II, Section 4 (emphasis added)(see Appendix A)
7. Fitschen, S.W. (President, National Legal Foundation), 10 <u>Regent University Law Review</u>, Spring, 1998, "Impeaching Federal Judges: A Covenental Constitutional Response to Judicial Tyranny" (citing 4 William Blackstone, <u>Commentaries on the Law of England</u>, at 121-123); <u>see also</u> en.wikipedia.org/wiki/High_crimes_and_misdemeanours, <u>Wikipedia Encyclopedia</u>, "High Crimes and Misdemeanours."
8. Levy, L.W., Karst, K.L. and Mahoney, D.J., <u>Encyclopedia of the American Constitution</u> (New York, MacMillan, 1986), "Impeachment," by Raoul Berger, at 958.
9. Rossiter, Clinton, <u>The Federalist Papers</u>, "Hamilton: No. 65,"(New York, Penguin Books, 1961) at 396

(emphasis added).

10. Rossiter (n. 9, <u>supra</u>), "Madison: No. 47," at 303 (italics in original) (underline added).

11. Rossiter (n. 9, <u>supra</u>), "Madison: No. 47," at 303 (emphasis added)

12. Rossiter (n. 9, <u>supra</u>), "No. 81: Hamilton," at 484-85 (italics and bold added).

13. <u>Clinton v. City of New York</u>, 524 U.S. 417, 450 (1998) (emphasis added).

14. U.S. Constitution, Article I, Clause 7 (emphasis added)(see Appendix A).

Chapter 12
None